WHERE IS THE WEALTH OF NATIONS?

WHERE IS THE WEALTH OF NATIONS?

Measuring Capital for the 21st Century

THE WORLD BANK
Washington, D.C.

1818 H Street, NW
Washington, DC 20433
Telephone 202-473-1000
Internet: www.worldbank.org
E-mail: feedback@worldbank.org

A publication of the World Bank.

2 3 4 09 08 07 06

Cover photo courtesy of Corbis.

Library of Congress Cataloging in Publication data has been applied for.

ISBN-10: 0-8213-6354-9
ISBN-13: 978-0-8213-6354-6
eISBN: 0-8213-6355-7
DOI: 10.1596/978-0-8213-6354-6

Table of Contents

FOREWORD

This volume asks a key question: Where is the Wealth of Nations? Answering this question yields important insights into the prospects for sustainable development in countries around the world. The estimates of total wealth–including produced, natural, and human and institutional capital–suggest that human capital and the value of institutions (as measured by rule of law) constitute the largest share of wealth in virtually all countries.

It is striking that natural capital constitutes a quarter of total wealth in low-income countries, greater than the share of produced capital. This suggests that better management of ecosystems and natural resources will be key to sustaining development while these countries build their infrastructure and human and institutional capital. Particularly noteworthy is the share of cropland and pastureland in the natural wealth of poor countries–at nearly 70 percent, this argues for a strong focus on efforts to sustain soil quality.

This new approach to capital also provides a comprehensive measure of changes in wealth, a key indicator of sustainability. There are important examples of resource-dependent countries, such as Botswana, that have used their natural resources to underpin impressive rates of growth. In addition, the research finds that the value of natural capital per person actually tends to rise with income when we look across countries–this contradicts the received wisdom that development necessarily entails the depletion of the environment.

However, the figures suggest that, per capita, most low-income countries have experienced declines in both total and natural capital. This is bad news not only from an environmental point of view, but also from a broader development perspective.

Growth is essential if developing countries are to meet the Millennium Development Goals by 2015. Growth, however, will be illusory if it is based on mining soils and depleting fisheries and forests. This report provides the indicators needed to manage the total portfolio of assets upon which development depends. Armed with this information, decision makers can direct the development process toward sustainable outcomes.

Ian Johnson
Vice President, Sustainable Development

François Bourguignon
Senior Vice President and Chief Economist

Acknowledgments

Where Is the Wealth of Nations? has been written by a team including Kirk Hamilton, Giovanni Ruta, Katharine Bolt, Anil Markandya, Suzette Pedroso-Galinato, Patricia Silva, M. Saeed Ordoubadi, Glenn-Marie Lange, and Liaila Tajibaeva. The estimation of wealth subcomponents is based on the background work of Susana Ferreira, Liying Zhou, Boon-Ling Yeo, and Roberto Martin-Hurtado.

The report received insightful comments from the peer reviewers, Marian Delos Angeles and Giles Atkinson. Specific contributions have been provided by Milen Dyoulgerov, Lidvard Gronnevet, and Per Ryden.

We are indebted to colleagues inside and outside the World Bank for providing useful feedback. Our thanks goes to Dina Abu-Ghaida, Dan Biller, Jan Bojo, Julia Bucknall, Richard Damania, John Dixon, Eric Fernandes, Alan Gelb, Alec Ian Gershberg, Tracy Hart, James Keith Hinchliffe, Julien Labonne, Kseniya Lvovsky, William Sutton, Walter Vergara, and Jian Xie.

The financial support of the Government of Sweden is acknowledged with gratitude.

This book is dedicated to the memory of David Pearce–professor, mentor, friend, and intellectual father of the work presented here.

Acronyms and Abbreviations

CES	constant elasticity of substitution
EA	environment accounts
eaNDP	environmentally adjusted net domestic product
ENRAP	Environment and Natural Resource Accounting Project
EPE	environmental protection expenditure
EU	European Union
Eurostat	European Commission's official statistical agency
FAO	Food and Agriculture Organization of the United Nations
GDP	gross domestic product
geNDP	greened economy net domestic product
GNI	gross national income
GNIPC	gross national income per capita
IO	input-output
IUCN	The World Conservation Union
MFA	material flow accounts
NAMEA	national accounting matrix including environmental accounts
NDP	net domestic product
NPV	net present value
PIM	perpetual inventory model
PPP	Purchasing Power Parities
PVC	Present Value of Change
OECD	Organisation for Economic Co-operation and Development
OLS	Ordinary Least Squares
SAM	social accounting matrix
SEEA	system of integrated environmental and economic accounting
SNA	system of national accounts
SNI	sustainable national income

SOEs	state-owned enterprises
SRRI	Social Rate of Return on Investment
TMR	total material requirements
UNEP-WCMC	United Nations Environment Programme World Conservation Monitoring Centre
WDI	World Development Indicators
WDPA	World Database of Protected Areas

Note: All dollar amounts are U.S. dollars unless otherwise indicated.

Looking for the Wealth of Nations—A Logical Map

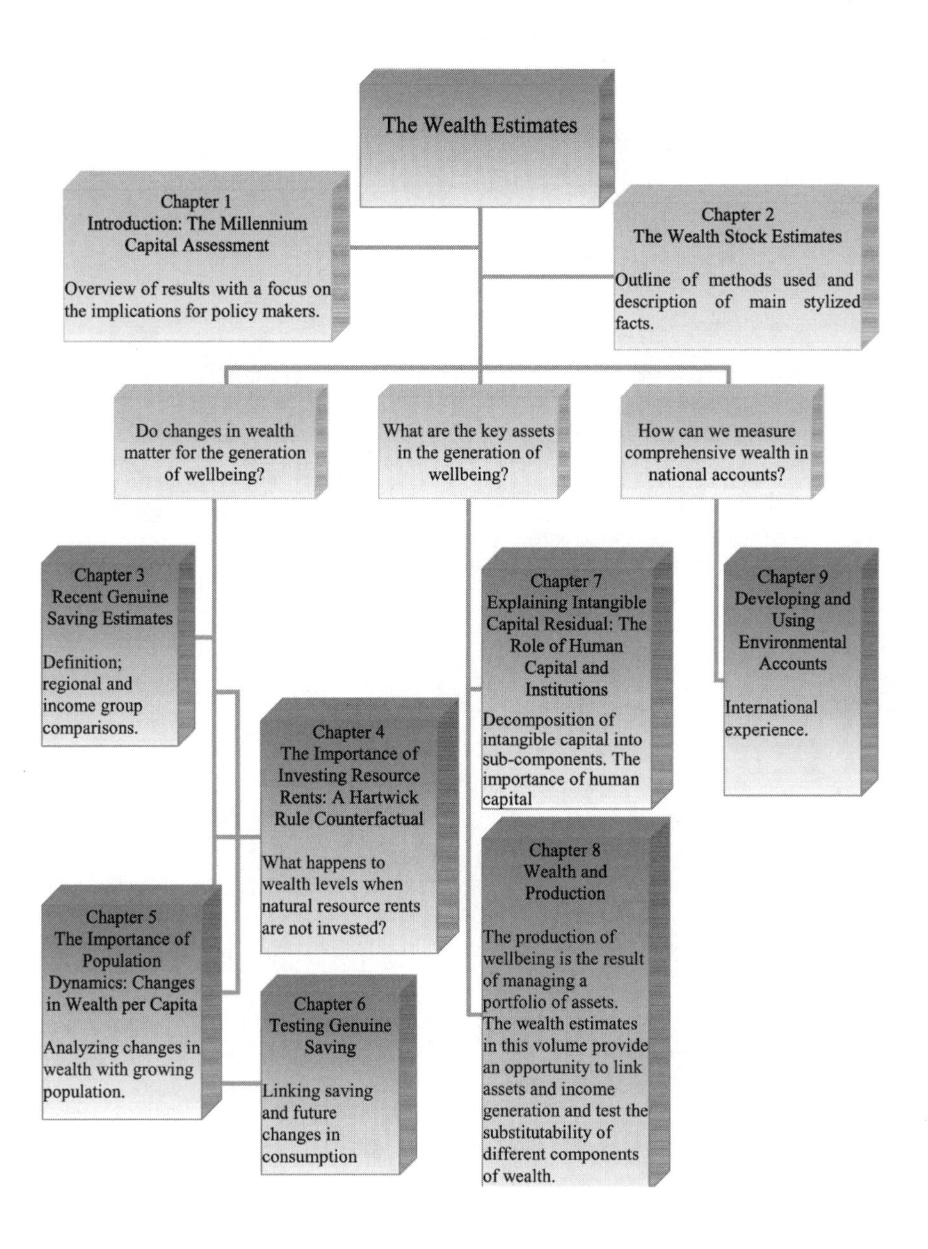

Executive Summary

With this volume, *Where Is the Wealth of Nations?* the World Bank publishes what could be termed the *millennium capital assessment:* monetary estimates of the range of assets—produced, natural, and intangible—upon which development depends. While important gaps remain, this comprehensive snapshot of wealth for 120 countries at the turn of the millennium aims to deepen our understanding of the linkages between development outcomes and the level and composition of wealth.

Figures 1 and 2 provide important insights into the role of natural resources in low-income countries (excluding *oil states* where resource rents exceed 20 percent of gross domestic product [GDP]). The first key message is that natural capital is an important share of total wealth, greater than the share of produced capital.[1] This suggests that managing natural resources must be a key part of development strategies. The composition of natural wealth in poor countries emphasizes the major role of agricultural land, but subsoil assets and timber and nontimber forest resources make up another quarter of total natural wealth.

The large share of natural resources in total wealth and the composition of these resources make a strong argument for the role of environmental resources in reducing poverty, fighting hunger, and lowering child

Figure 1 Shares of Total Wealth in Low-Income Countries, 2000

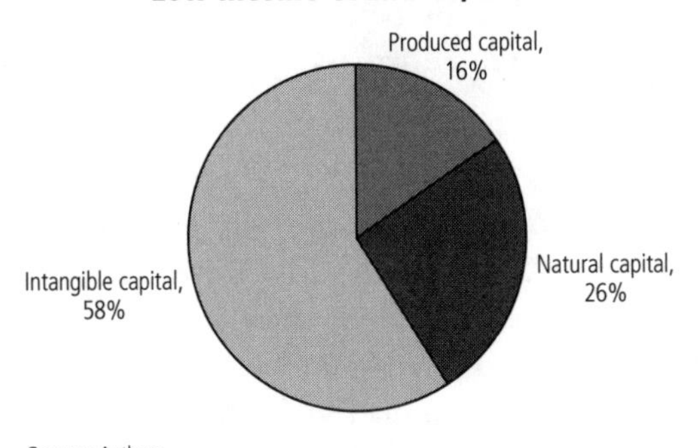

Source: Authors.
Note: Oil states excluded.

Figure 2 Shares of Natural Wealth in Low-Income Countries, 2000

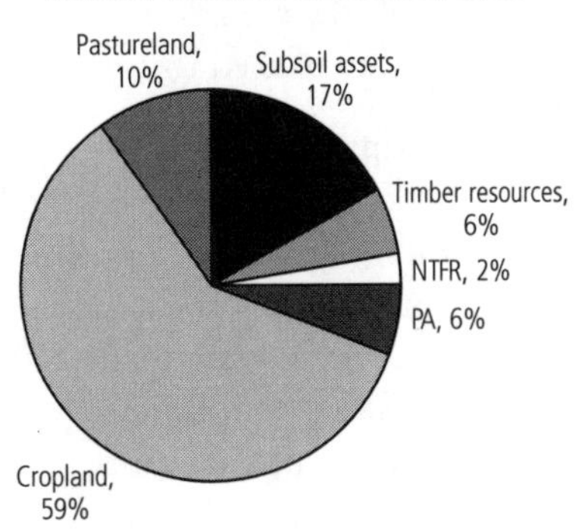

Source: Authors.
Note: Oil states excluded.
NTFR: Nontimber forest resources. PA: Protected areas.

mortality. The analysis in this volume proceeds from an overview of the wealth of nations to analyze the key role of the management of wealth through saving and investments. It also analyzes the importance of human capital and good governance and engages finance ministries in developing a comprehensive agenda that looks at natural resources as an integral part of their policy domain.

Where Is the Wealth of Nations? is organized around three key questions. Each chapter tackles a particular aspect of the wealth-wellbeing equation and describes the story behind the numbers and the relative policy implications. Before engaging the key issues, chapter 1 and chapter 2 introduce the reader into the structure, results, and main policy implications of the volume.

Chapter 1 provides an overview of the wealth estimates with a focus on the implications for policy makers. It introduces the notion of development as a process of portfolio management—a powerful framework for action. Certain assets in the portfolio are exhaustible and can only be transformed into other assets through investment of the resource rents. Other assets are renewable and can yield sustainable income streams. Economic analysis can guide decisions concerning the optimal size of these assets in the portfolio.

The wealth estimates suggest that the preponderant form of wealth worldwide is intangible capital—human capital and the quality of formal and informal institutions. Moreover, the share of produced assets in total wealth is virtually constant across income groups, with a moderate increase in produced capital intensiveness in middle-income countries. The share of natural capital in total wealth tends to fall with income, while the share of intangible capital rises. The latter point makes perfect sense—rich countries are largely rich because of the skills of their populations and the quality of the institutions supporting economic activity.

Chapter 2 takes the reader through the methodology used to estimate wealth, explaining the methods and assumptions used. The total wealth estimates reported in *Where Is the Wealth of Nations?* are built upon a combination of top-down and bottom-up approaches. Total wealth, in line with economic theory, is estimated as the present value of future consumption. Produced capital stocks are derived from historical investment data using a perpetual inventory model (PIM). Natural resource stock values are based upon country-level data on physical stocks and estimates of natural resource rents based on world prices and local costs. Intangible capital, then, is measured as the difference between total wealth and the other produced and natural stocks. The estimates of natural wealth are limited by data—fish stocks and subsoil water are not measured in the estimates—while the environmental services that underpin human societies and economies are not measured explicitly.

The introduction of the wealth estimates methodology and results in the first two chapters sets the stage for the three leading questions in the volume. The central tenet of *Where Is the Wealth of Nations?* is embodied in chapters 4 through 7. While wealth composition may, to some extent, determine the development options available to a particular country, the quality of development depends crucially on how wealth changes over time. Natural capital can be transformed into other forms of capital, provided resource rents are efficiently invested.

Do Changes in Wealth Matter for the Generation of Well-Being?

Natural resources are special economic goods because they are not produced. As a consequence, natural resources will yield economic profits—rents—if properly managed. These rents can be an important source of development finance, and countries like Botswana and Malaysia have successfully used natural resources in this way. There are no sustainable diamond mines, but there are sustainable diamond-mining countries. Behind this statement is an assumption that it is possible to transform one form of wealth—diamonds in the ground—into other forms of wealth such as buildings, machines, and human capital.

Saving is obviously a core aspect of development. Without the creation of a surplus for investment there is no way for countries to escape a low-level subsistence equilibrium. Resource dependence complicates the measurement of saving effort because depletion of natural resources is not visible in standard national accounts. Adjusted net or *genuine* saving measures the true level of saving in a country after depreciation of produced capital; investments in human capital (as measured by education expenditures); depletion of minerals, energy, and forests; and damages from local and global air pollutants are taken into account. Chapter 3 describes the estimation of adjusted net saving. It then goes on to present and discuss the empirical calculations of genuine saving rates available for over 140 countries.

Development has been referred to as a *process of portfolio management.* The Hartwick rule for sustainability actually mandates that in order to achieve sustainable consumption, countries should invest their rents from natural resources. Drawing on a 30-year time series of resource rent data underlying the adjusted net saving estimates, chapter 4 constructs a Hartwick rule counterfactual: how rich would countries be in the year 2000 if they had followed the Hartwick rule since 1970? The empirical estimations in this chapter test two variants of the Hartwick rule—the standard rule, which amounts to keeping genuine saving precisely equal to zero at each point in time, and a version that assumes a constant level of positive genuine saving at each point in time. In many cases, the results are striking. The calculations show how even a moderate saving effort, equivalent to the average saving effort of the poorest countries in the world, could have substantially increased the wealth of resource-dependent economies. In 2000, Nigeria, a major oil exporter, could have had a stock of produced capital five times higher. Moreover, if these investments had taken place, oil would play a much smaller role in the Nigerian economy today, with likely beneficial impacts on policies affecting other sectors of the economy. Republica Bolivariana de Venezuela could have four times as much produced capital. In per capita terms, the economies of the Republica Bolivariana de Venezuela, Trinidad and Tobago, and Gabon, all rich in petroleum, could today have a stock of produced capital of roughly US$30,000 per person, comparable to the Republic of Korea.

Adjusted net saving is introduced in chapter 3 as a more inclusive measure of net saving effort. Yet, if population is not static, then it is clearly per capita welfare that policy should aim to sustain. While adjusted net saving is answering an important question—did total wealth rise or fall over the accounting period?—it does not speak directly to the question of the sustainability of economies when there is a growing population. This task is undertaken in chapter 5. If genuine saving is negative, then it is clear in both total and per capita terms that wealth is declining. For a range of countries, however, it is possible that genuine saving in total could be positive while wealth per capita is declining. Countries with high population growth rates are effectively on a treadmill and need to create new wealth just to maintain existing levels of wealth per capita. In general, the results suggest very large saving gaps in Sub-Saharan Africa when population growth is taken into account. Excluding the oil states, saving gaps (the increase in saving required to maintain current levels of wealth per capita) in many countries are on the order of 10 percent to 50 percent of the gross national income (GNI). Against this must be set the realization that reigning in government consumption by even a few percentage points of GNI is extremely painful and often politically perilous. Macroeconomic policies alone seem unlikely to close the gap.

Economic theory suggests that current net saving should equal the change in future well-being, specifically the present value of future changes in consumption. Chapter 6 tests this hypothesis. The saving tests using historical data reported in this volume suggest that a particular variant of genuine saving, one that excludes education expenditures, damage from carbon dioxide emissions, and the immiserating effects of population growth, is a good predictor of future changes in well-being. Genuine saving is, therefore, a potentially important indicator to guide development policy. The analysis includes a further key result: when the sample of countries is limited to high-income countries, there is no apparent empirical relationship between current net saving and future well-being. This raises an important distinction between developed and developing countries. It says quite clearly that asset accumulation, the apparent driver of future welfare when all countries are tested, is not a significant factor in rich countries. This result makes eminent sense. In the richest countries it is clear that technological change, institutional innovation, learning by doing, and social capital, to name a few factors, are fundamental drivers of the economy.

While saving is at the basis of sustainable development, the composition of wealth determines the menu of options a given government has available. The second key question looks at specific types of wealth and their role.

What Are the Key Assets in the Generation of Well-Being?

As pointed out, most of a country's wealth is captured by what we term intangible capital. Given its importance, chapter 7 deals with the decomposition of intangible capital into subcomponents. By construction, the intangible capital variable captures all those assets that are unaccounted for in the estimates of produced and natural capital. Intangible assets include the skills and know-how embodied in the labor force. The category also includes social capital, that is, the trust among people in a society and their ability to work together for a common purpose. The residual also accounts for all those governance elements that boost the productivity of labor. For example, if an economy has a very efficient judicial system, clear property rights, and an effective government, the effects will result in a higher total wealth and thus a higher *intangible capital* residual. The regression analysis in this chapter shows that human capital and rule of law account for the majority of the variation in the residual. Investments in education, the functioning of the justice system, and policies aimed at attracting remittances are the most important means of increasing the intangible components of total wealth.

In chapter 2 it is observed that as countries become richer, the relative importance of produced and intangible assets rises in ratio to natural assets. Thus, the development process primarily entails growth in the *modern* sectors of manufacturing and services, which depend heavily on more intangible forms of wealth. Yet, the value of natural resources per person does not decline as income rises, particularly for agricultural land. Chapter 8 tests the hypothesis that land and other natural resources are, in fact, key in sustaining income generation. Underlying any wealth accounts is an implicit *production function,* which is a blueprint of the combinations of different assets with which we can achieve a given level of output. These blueprints are usually written as a mathematical function, which describes the precise relationship between the availability of different amounts of inputs, such as physical and human capital services, and the maximum output they could produce. The substitutability between inputs is then measured as an *elasticity of substitution*. The results provide some interesting findings. There is no sign that the elasticity of substitution between the natural resource (land) and other inputs is particularly low. Wherever land emerges as a significant input, it has an elasticity of substitution approximately equal to or greater than one. This outcome, on one hand, confirms that countries' opportunities are not necessarily dictated by their endowments of natural resources. On the other hand, it validates the importance of a Hartwick rule of saving the rents from the exploitation of natural resources if we are to achieve a sustained level of income generation.

How Can Comprehensive Wealth and Its Changes Be Measured in National Accounts?

A central tenet of the volume is the need for a pragmatic vision of sustainable development as a process of administering a portfolio of assets. Having committed themselves to achieving sustainable development, governments face a number of challenges beyond the traditional concerns of their natural resources and environmental agencies. Policy makers setting environmental standards need to be aware of the likely consequences for the economy, while economic policy makers must consider the sustainability of current and projected patterns of production and consumption. Such integration and adoption of the notion of sustainable development by governments have been the motivation for developing environmental accounting. Chapter 9 provides a context to explore the usefulness of the system of environmental and economic accounts (SEEA) as an operational framework for monitoring sustainability and its policy use. The chapter summarizes the four general components of the environmental accounts. Furthermore, it reviews a few policy applications of environmental accounting in industrialized and developing countries, and also indicates potential applications, which may not be fully exploited at this time.

Putting It All Together

It is in developing countries where accounting based on comprehensive wealth and its changes is most likely to be a useful indicator to guide policy. The evidence in this volume suggests that investments in produced capital, human capital, and governance, combined with saving efforts aimed at offsetting the depletion of natural resources, can lead to future welfare increases in developing countries.

The step from saving to investment is crucially important. If investments are not profitable, the effect on wealth is equivalent to consumption, but without the boost to well-being presumed to accompany consumption.

Achieving the transition from natural-resource dependence to a sustained and balanced growth requires a set of institutions that are capable of managing the natural resource, collecting resource rents, and directing these rents into profitable investments. Resource policy, fiscal policy, and political economy all have a role to play in this transformation.

Endnote

1. The largest share, intangible capital, consists of an amalgam of human capital, governance, and other factors that are difficult to value explicitly.

PART 1

WEALTH ACCOUNTING

Chapter 1

Introduction: The Millennium Capital Assessment

Can poverty reduction be sustained? The end of the 20th century saw a renewed commitment to ending poverty embodied in the Millennium Development Goals. However, deep concerns remained that current rates of depletion and degradation of natural resources may undermine any progress achieved. Achieving sustainable outcomes will require sustaining the total wealth—produced, human, natural—on which development depends.

Building on several years of effort, including *Expanding the Measure of Wealth* (World Bank 1997), this volume assesses the wealth of the planet in the year 2000. In speaking of *wealth* we are returning to the ideas of the classical economists, who viewed land, labor, and produced capital as the primary factors of production. The chapters that follow detail the levels and changes in these different productive factors across the developing and the developed worlds.

This volume represents the most recent achievement in a long-term program to estimate wealth and its components for a large set of countries. It improves the work in *Expanding the Measure of Wealth* by extending country coverage and by basing the estimation of produced capital and natural capital on a broader set of data. Details on the estimation procedure are provided in appendix 1, while box 1.1 gives a basic exposition of the theory underlying this book.

The composition of wealth varies considerably by region and particularly by level of income. While this disparity may be obvious in comparing a mental image of, say, Malawi and Sweden, subsequent chapters measure this variation rigorously by providing figures for nearly 120 countries on the per capita values of agricultural land, minerals, forests, produced assets, and an aggregate[1] termed *intangible capital.* Intangible capital includes raw labor, human capital, social capital, and other factors such as the quality of institutions. Tables 1.1 and 1.2[2] present the big picture on the composition and levels of wealth per capita by income group and for the world as a whole.[3]

Table 1.1 Total Wealth, 2000

— $ per capita and percentage shares —

Income group	Natural capital	Produced capital	Intangible capital	Total wealth	Natural capital share	Produced capital share	Intangible capital share
Low-income countries	1,925	1,174	4,434	7,532	26%	16%	59%
Middle-income countries	3,496	5,347	18,773	27,616	13%	19%	68%
High-income OECD countries	9,531	76,193	353,339	439,063	2%	17%	80%
World	4,011	16,850	74,998	95,860	4%	18%	78%

Source: Authors.

Notes: All dollars at nominal exchange rates. Oil states are excluded. OECD: Organisation for Economic Co-operation and Development

Table 1.2 Natural Capital, 2000

— $ per capita —

Income group	Subsoil assets	Timber resources	NTFR	Protected Areas	Cropland	Pastureland	Total natural capital
Low-income countries	325	109	48	111	1,143	189	1,925
Middle-income countries	1,089	169	120	129	1,583	407	3,496
High-income countries (OECD)	3,825	747	183	1,215	2,008	1,552	9,531
World	1,302	252	104	322	1,496	536	4,011

Source: Authors.

Notes: NTFR: Nontimber forest resources. Oil states are excluded.

If development is approached as a process of portfolio management, then the figures make clear that both the size and composition of the portfolio vary hugely across levels of income. Managing each component of the portfolio well and transforming one form of asset into another most efficiently are key facets of development policy.

Changes in real wealth determine future prospects for well-being. Accordingly, an important element of the analysis that follows is the measurement of *adjusted net* or *genuine* saving. Estimated saving rates for over 140 countries show that rates of wealth accumulation are much higher in proportion to gross national income (GNI) in rich countries than in poor countries. This is particularly the case when population growth is factored into the analysis. Evidence suggests that higher natural resource dependence coincides with lower genuine saving rates. Chapters 3 and 5 detail these results.

While the analysis of wealth sheds light on sustainability, it is also directly relevant to the question of growth. Growth is essential if the poorest countries are to enjoy increases in well-being. However, growth will be illusory if it consists primarily of consuming the assets, such as soil nutrients, that underpin the economy.

The linkage between measured changes in real wealth and future well-being only holds if our measures of wealth are suitably comprehensive. This is the prime motivation for expanding the measure of wealth to include a range of natural and intangible capital. This richer picture of the asset base also opens the door to a range of policy interventions that can increase and sustain growth.

Where Is the Wealth of Nations?

The total wealth estimates reported here are built upon a combination of top-down and bottom-up approaches. These are presented briefly in the next chapter and detailed in appendix 1. Total wealth, in line with economic theory, is estimated as the present value of future consumption. Produced capital stocks are derived from historical investment data using a perpetual inventory model (PIM).[4] Natural resource stock values are based upon country-level data on physical stocks, and estimates of natural resource rents are based on world prices and local costs. Intangible capital then is measured as the difference between total wealth and the other produced and natural stocks.

While table 1.1 reports an average global wealth per capita of roughly $96,000, this average clearly masks huge variety. The results by income group are more informative.

Total wealth per capita clearly varies significantly between developed and developing countries.[5] Beyond these large ratios are three other facts displayed in table 1.1:

- The share of produced assets in total wealth is virtually constant across income groups.
- The share of natural capital in total wealth tends to fall with income, while the share of intangible capital rises.
- The value of natural capital per capita is substantially higher in rich countries than in poor, while the share of wealth is much lower.

The wealth estimates suggest that the preponderant form of wealth is intangible capital, an expected result and an insight that goes back at least to Adam Smith.[6] A huge variation in intangible capital per capita occurs across income levels. Taking the ratio of intangible capital to produced capital offers a different insight: this ratio varies from 3.8 in low-income countries to 3.5 in middle-income and 4.6 in high-income—a rather small variation. This suggests that over the course of economic development intangible capital and produced capital are accumulated roughly in the same proportion, with a tendency toward produced capital intensiveness at middle-income levels and intangible capital intensiveness at high-income levels.

Does the 2 percent share of natural capital in total wealth for high-income countries mean that natural resources are somehow unimportant in these countries? Table 1.2 suggests not. Per capita values of each of the natural resource categories—subsoil assets, timber and nontimber resources, protected areas, and agricultural land—are higher in rich countries than in poor. What the low natural-capital share suggests is that the development process primarily entails growth in the modern sectors of manufacturing and services, while the primary sectors are relatively static. The estimates of natural wealth presented in this book are also limited by data—for example, fish stocks are not measured in the estimates, while the environmental services that underpin human societies and economies are not measured explicitly.

Natural Resources and Development

Natural resources are special economic goods because they are not produced. As a consequence, natural resources will yield economic profits—rents—if properly managed. These rents can be an important source of development finance, and countries like Botswana and Malaysia have successfully leveraged natural resources in this way.

There are no sustainable diamond mines, but there are sustainable diamond-mining countries. Implicit in this statement is the assumption that it is possible to transform one form of wealth—diamonds in the ground—into other forms of wealth, such as buildings, machines, and human capital. Achieving this transformation requires a set of institutions capable of managing the natural resource, collecting resource rents, and directing these rents into profitable investments. Resource policy, fiscal policy, political factors, institutions, and governance structure all have a role to play in this transformation.

Exhaustible resources, once discovered, can only be depleted. Consuming rents from exhaustible resources is, therefore, literally consuming capital, which motivates the Hartwick policy rule for sustaining development—invest resource rents in other forms of capital.

Living resources are unique because they are a potentially sustainable source of resource rents—truly a gift of nature. Sustainable management of these resources will be the optimal policy, but the question of the optimal stock size is complex. For example, clearing forest land for agriculture will be optimal up to the point where the land rent on the marginal cleared hectare is just equal to the total economic value of the standing forest.[7]

Land resources are potentially sustainable if managed well. Land is particularly important in the poorest countries because it is a direct source of livelihood and sustenance for many poor households. As table 1.2 shows, cropland and pastureland make up 70 percent of natural wealth in low-income countries and 18 percent of total wealth.

Natural resources play two basic roles in development:

- The first, mostly applicable to the poorest countries and poorest communities, is the role of local natural resources as the basis of subsistence.
- The second is as a source of development finance. Commercial natural resources can be important sources of profit and foreign exchange. Rents on exhaustible, renewable, and potentially sustainable resources can be used to finance investments in other forms of wealth. In the case of exhaustible resources these rents *must* be invested if total wealth is not to decline.

While the preceding discussion has focused on natural *goods,* chapter 3 will also show the importance of measuring environmental *bads* in the form of marginal damages from local and global air pollutants. Pollution, which does not appear directly in the wealth stock estimates, is included implicitly in the form of lowered labor productivity linked to ill health. This depresses income generation, limiting consumption, and accordingly, total wealth.

From a development perspective a key message from table 1.1 is that natural resources make up a very significant share of the total wealth in low-income countries—26 percent—and that this is substantially larger than the share of produced capital. Sound management of these natural resources can support and sustain the welfare of poor countries, and poor people in poor countries, as they move up the development ladder.

Policies and Institutions

A major focus in this analysis is on placing economic values on stocks of natural resources and changes in the values of these stocks. This information is used to illuminate the role that natural resources play in development, particularly in poor countries. The analysis suggests that changes in natural resource management are needed to increase economic benefits, and the need for these changes will lead to reforms of policies and institutions.

From an economic perspective, inefficiencies in resource exploitation can potentially take the form of under- or overexploitation. In practice, incentives for resource management generally encourage excess exploitation, which will depress genuine saving relative to its level under efficient exploitation. Reforming resource management practices can play a significant role in boosting saving levels in highly resource-dependent economies.

Extensive literature exists on policies and institutions for natural resource management, dealing with the very different problems of open- or common-access, exploiting exhaustible resources such as minerals and energy, and managing living resources such as forests and fish. This literature thoroughly explores the roles that different types of policy instruments, property rights, and institutional structures can play in ensuring efficient resource management. This study will not attempt to summarize or add significantly to this literature.

However, an important set of institutions—ministries of finance and treasury—often overlooks the analysis of natural resource issues. The fiscal policy implications of natural resource management in developing countries will be explored below.

Saving and Investment

Saving is a core aspect of development. Without the creation of a surplus for investment, there is no way for countries to escape a state of low-level subsistence.

Adjusted net or genuine saving measures the true level of saving in a country after accounting for depreciation of produced capital; investments in human capital (as measured by education expenditures); depletion of minerals, energy, and forests; and damages from local and global air pollutants. Economic theory suggests that current net saving should equal the change in future welfare, specifically the present value of future changes in consumption (Hamilton and Hartwick 2005).

Resource dependence complicates the measurement of saving effort because a depletion of natural resources often occurs but is not visible in standard national accounts. As will be seen in chapter 3, the dissaving associated with resource depletion is a particular problem in low-income countries.

The saving tests using historical data reported in chapter 6 suggest that a particular variant of genuine saving—one that excludes education expenditures, damage from carbon dioxide emissions, and the immiserating effects of population growth—is a good predictor of future changes in welfare. Genuine saving is therefore an important indicator to guide development policy.

Saving in Developed and Developing Countries

The analysis in chapter 6 includes a further key result: When the sample of countries is limited to high-income countries, there is no apparent empirical relationship between current net saving and future welfare. This raises an important distinction between developed and developing countries. It says quite clearly that asset accumulation, the apparent driver of future welfare when all countries are tested, is not a significant factor in rich countries. This result makes eminent sense—in the richest countries it is clear that technological change, institutional innovation, learning by doing, and efficient institutions, to name a few factors, are fundamental drivers of growth.

It is in developing countries, therefore, where genuine saving is most likely to be a useful indicator to guide policy. As chapters 3 and 5 will show, the poorest countries have the lowest genuine saving rates. The tests of genuine saving suggest that investments in produced capital, combined with saving efforts aimed at offsetting the depletion of natural resources, can lead to future welfare increases in developing countries.

Finally, the step from saving to investment is crucially important. If investments are not profitable, the effect on wealth is equivalent to consumption, but without the boost to well-being presumed to accompany consumption.

Fiscal Policy and Comprehensive Wealth

Expanding the measure of wealth to include natural resources raises an important set of fiscal issues concerning revenues, expenditures, fiscal space, boom-and-bust cycles, and the quasi-fiscal impact of state-owned enterprises (SOEs). Dealing with these issues will not likely turn finance ministers into environmentalists, but a sharper focus on the fiscal aspects of natural resources can have a substantial impact on macrobalances and economic performance in many countries.

Revenue issues with respect to commercial natural resources are well understood. The government, as the owner of the resource, should be taxing natural resource rents to the point where the private sector is just willing to risk capital in natural resource exploitation. This applies equally to minerals, forests, and fisheries. For forests and fisheries there is the additional concern with sustainability: if sectoral policies encourage overexploitation of the resource, then fiscal revenues from the sector may not be sustained. Finally, there is the issue of rent capture from foreign tourists. If a country's natural resources attract foreign tourists, then taxes on entry and hotels are important instruments for resource rent capture.

For government *expenditures* major questions revolve around the use of resource revenues. In principle, the government should seek to reinvest royalties on exhaustible resources in other assets—thereby maintaining the total wealth of the nation. The caveat to this basic rule is that public investments must be profitable. The issue of profitability may raise questions of absorptive capacity—the capacity of governments to make productive investments—which is typically constrained by the availability of factors such as skilled labor and infrastructure. Countries with significant debts have the option of investing resource rents in debt reduction. Whether this is a good investment depends on the social returns to the best alternative project. In addition, certain types of development expenditures, for example, on national parks, may not appear to be particularly profitable from the treasury's viewpoint; a broader view, though, may suggest that investments in parks will increase tourist sector growth and increase fiscal revenues from tourists.

The phenomenon of *fiscal boom-and-bust* is common for many resource exporters where government revenues are highly dependent on resource royalties. *Easy money* in the form of resource revenues tempts governments to increase consumption expenditures when commodity prices are buoyant. These expenditures are often difficult to rein in when the inevitable commodity bust arrives, leading to major fiscal imbalances. Generally, investing resource rents requires a system to help governments stabilize resource revenues, as well as instruments, such as medium-term expenditure frameworks, to control expenditures.

Comprehensive wealth accounts offer new insights into the question of *fiscal space,* that is, the ability of the government to increase expenditure without jeopardizing its ability to service its debt. Generally, the measure of a government's change in fiscal stance is the change in its net worth. This suggests that tax revenues from exhaustible resources do not fully increase fiscal space because a portion of these taxes represents the consumption of natural capital. While the news that fiscal space is not as large as conventionally measured will not be welcomed by most treasuries, prudent governments will heed the bad news.

SOEs are common in the resource sectors and present *quasi-fiscal* risks of their own. The low efficiency of these enterprises may lead to the growth of liabilities. If the enterprises are off-budget, then these contingent fiscal liabilities are typically not factored into the government's fiscal stance. If the enterprises are on-budget, then they often do not have retained earnings out of which to finance capital expenditures; the result is that the investment needs of the SOE become part of the government development budget. In this case there is a risk of undercapitalization of SOEs.

Botswana provides an example of sound management of many of these fiscal issues with respect to its diamond wealth. The treasury calculates a sustainable budget index to determine whether consumption expenditures are being financed out of resource rents and adjusts expenditures accordingly. It also holds diamond revenues offshore in order to deal with issues of absorptive capacity, revenue stabilization, and Dutch disease effects from currency appreciation.

Investing in the Intangible Capital Residual

From a policy perspective a potential problem may arise with calculating such a large intangible capital residual. Since the residual necessarily includes a wide array of less-tangible assets—for example, raw labor, human capital, social capital, or quality of institutions—it raises the question of whether virtually *any* component of public spending could be considered to be a type of investment. To explore this question using cross-sectional data, chapter 7 estimates the major factors contributing to the intangible capital residual, and tables 1.3 and 1.4 present some key results.

Table 1.3 Factors Explaining the Intangible Capital Residual

Factor	Elasticity		
School years per capita	0.53	R-squared	0.89
Rule of law index	0.83		
Remittances per capita	0.12		

Source: Authors.
Note: Coefficients are significant at the 5 percent level.

Table 1.4 Marginal Returns to Different Factors

Income group	School years per capita	Rule of law index	Remittances per capita
Low-income countries	838	111	29
Middle-income countries	1,954	404	39
High-income countries (OECD)	16,430	2,973	306

Source: Authors.
Note: Figures represent the increase in the intangible capital residual associated with a 1-unit increase in the given factor.

Any model of the intangible residual must include only factors that are not already captured in the value of produced capital and natural resources, since these have been subtracted from total wealth in order to calculate the residual. Table 1.3 shows that three such factors—average years of schooling per capita, rule of law, and remittances received per capita—explain 89 percent of the total variation in the residual across countries.

Policy makers, therefore, can be reasonably confident that investments in education and the justice system, as well as policies aimed at attracting remittances, are the most important means of increasing the intangible-capital component of total wealth. The elasticities reported in table 1.3 show that, on average, for all countries a 1 percent increase in rule of law pays large dividends, boosting intangible capital by 0.83 percent; 1 percent increases in the stock of schooling or remittances per capita will increase intangible capital by 0.53 percent and 0.12 percent, respectively.

Table 1.4 reports the marginal returns, measured at the mean, to unit increases in the three factors for each level of income. Increasing the average stock of schooling by one year per person increases total wealth per capita by nearly $840 in low-income countries; nearly $2,000 in middle-income countries; and over $16,000 in high-income countries. The wide range reflects the *gearing* effect of having larger stocks of produced capital at higher-income levels, as well as the use of nominal exchange rates. A one-point increase in the rule of law index (on a 100-point scale) boosts total wealth by over $100 in low-income countries, over $400 in middle-income countries, and nearly $3,000 in high-income countries.

Setting aside the smallest factor, remittances, it is worth considering how finance ministries can invest in the factors explaining the intangible capital aggregate. Education expenditure can obviously play a role, but these expenditures have to be effective in actually creating human capital. Investing in rule of law is clearly complex. Issues of judicial salaries, for example, can be important. However, the larger problem is building trusted, competent legal institutions, thereby creating confidence in the minds of citizens and entrepreneurs that their rights will be protected. The returns to doing so, reported in chapter 7, are potentially very large.

Conclusions

The notion of development as portfolio management is powerful. Certain assets in the portfolio are exhaustible and can only be transformed into other productive assets, such as infrastructure or human capital, through investment of the resource rents. Other assets are renewable and can yield sustainable income streams. Economic analysis can guide decisions concerning the optimal size of these assets in the portfolio. Some assets, such as produced capital, depreciate over time. National savings can be used to invest in natural assets, produced capital, or human capital. The choice of investment will depend on the asset with the highest marginal return on investment, a standard tenet of public finance.

Each year from 10 to 20 developing countries have negative genuine saving rates. What should the policy response be? Monetary and fiscal policies affect saving behavior, and public sector dissaving can be a key target of policy. If investment in human capital is measured as saving, then efforts to increase effective education expenditures can boost overall saving. For natural resources the general prescription is not to simply reduce exploitation, but rather to reduce incentives for overexploitation, which will typically entail reforms in the resource sectors.

The evidence presented in subsequent chapters shows that low or negative saving is primarily an issue in low-income countries and some resource-dependent middle-income countries. For resource-dependent middle-income countries, negative saving is almost always a reflection of excessive government consumption expenditure. Conversely, for the poorest countries a prescription to boost saving by reducing consumption is clearly unpalatable. A better policy response is to boost the productivity of all assets, including resource assets, in these countries through policy and institutional reforms, leading to a cycle of rising consumption and saving.

BOX 1.1 The Theory of Wealth, Welfare, and Sustainable Development

Wealth, welfare, and sustainability are closely interlinked. Pezzey (1989) suggested a straightforward definition of sustainability: a development path is sustainable if utility does not decline at any point along the path. Dasgupta (2001) offers a more general definition: a development path is sustainable if *social welfare* does not decline at any point along the path. Social welfare is in turn defined to be the present value of utility along the development path—it is a measure of intertemporal wellbeing.

While a useful concept, utility is not directly observable. This raises a measurement challenge: can we define an index of measurable quantities that can be shown to be related to social welfare? The suggestion that *total wealth* can provide such a measure is presented in Samuelson (1961): "...the only valid approximation to a measure of welfare comes from computing *wealth-like* magnitudes not income magnitudes." According to Samuelson, the work of Irving Fisher (1906) pointed the way: current wealth should equal the present value of future consumption. Hamilton and Hartwick (2005) show that the sum of the values of a heterogeneous set of assets (total wealth) is equal to the present value of future consumption. These notions of wealth and welfare underpin the basic calculation of total wealth in this book.

It follows that if total wealth is related to social welfare, then changes in wealth should have implications for sustainability—this is the basic intuition of Pearce and Atkinson (1993). For optimal economies, economies where a planner can enforce the maximization of social welfare, a number of results have made the link explicit (it is implicit in Weitzman [1976], but not derived). Aronsson and others (1997, equation 6.18) show that net saving in utility units is equal to the present value of changes in utility, using a time-varying pure rate of time preference. Hamilton and Clemens (1999) show that net or 'genuine' saving adjusted for resource depletion, stock pollutant damages, and human capital accumulation is equal to the change in social welfare measured in dollars; they also establish that negative genuine saving implies that future utility must be less than current utility over some interval of time. This motivates the focus on savings in chapter 3 below.

These results depend on the assumption that governments maximize social welfare. Dasgupta and Mäler (2000) show that net investment is equal to the change in social welfare in a nonoptimizing framework where a resource allocation mechanism is used to specify the mapping from initial capital stocks to future stocks and flows in the economy. This result depends on accounting prices for assets being defined as the marginal changes in social welfare resulting from an increment in each asset (that is, accounting prices are the partial derivatives of the social welfare function). Arrow and others (2003a) explore the accounting issues under a variety of resource allocation mechanisms.

In this book resource stocks and resource depletion are valued using world prices and local costs of extraction and harvest. The use of border prices is consistent with how projects would be evaluated using social cost-benefit analysis, but it is not explicitly linked either to assumptions about optimality or to any specific resource allocation mechanism as in Dasgupta and Mäler (2000).

Hartwick (1977) provided the canonical rule for sustainability in resource-dependent economies–if genuine saving is set equal to zero at each point in time (that is, traditional net saving just equals resource depletion), then consumption can be maintained indefinitely, even in the face of finite resources and fixed technology. Hamilton and others (forthcoming) show that this can be generalized to a rule with constant positive genuine saving; such a rule will yield unbounded consumption. Chapter 4 calculates countries' produced capital stocks under the alternative Hartwick rules during 1970–2000; these calculations are then compared with actual year 2000 capital stocks.

If population grows over time, as in virtually all developing countries, then changes in total wealth should take into account the change in population. Dasgupta (2001) shows that wealth per capita is the correct measure of social welfare if certain conditions are met: (i) population grows at a constant rate; (ii) per capita consumption is independent of population size; and (iii) production exhibits constant returns to scale. This book calculates wealth per capita as the measure of social well-being under these assumptions, as do Arrow and others (2004). The measure of the change in wealth per capita derived in chapter 5 below includes a specific adjustment for the immiserating effects of population growth. Arrow and others (2003b) identify the correct welfare index in more general situations.

Finally, the result linking net saving to changes in social welfare in Aronsson and others (1997) can be extended to show that current saving equals the present value of changes in consumption in an optimizing economy. Dasgupta (2001) shows that the same is true in nonoptimal economies where accounting prices are defined as above. Hamilton and Hartwick (2005) show that this relationship holds in an optimal economy, but their proof clearly only requires that the economy be competitive. This relationship between current saving and the present value of future changes in consumption is exploited in an empirical test of genuine saving in chapter 6.

Endnotes

1. Intangible capital includes raw labor, human capital, social capital, and other important factors such as the quality of institutions.

2. All references to dollars ($) are in U.S. dollars.

3. Oil states (where oil rents exceed 20 percent of GNI) are excluded and are discussed separately in later chapters. The very large resource endowments of these countries make them outliers in the analysis of wealth.

4. Pritchett (2000) argues that cumulating investments in this way is likely to overstate the value of capital stocks in developing countries, because the method does not account for the profitability of these investments.

5. The use of nominal exchange rates explains part of the high variation. Purchasing Power Parities (PPP) are typically used to compare welfare between developed and developing countries. Welfare measurement is not the prime concern in this volume, where the focus is on variation in the composition of wealth across income levels, changes in wealth, and the role of natural assets in development.

6. In *An Inquiry into the Nature and Causes of the Wealth of Nations,* Adam Smith (1776) wrote: "The annual labour of every nation is the fund which originally supplies it with all the necessaries and conveniences of life which it annually consumes." Smith recognized "the skill, dexterity, and judgment with which [. . .] labour is generally applied" as a precondition for generating supply "whatever be the soil, climate, or extent of territory of any particular nation."

7. Total economic value in this instance would include the rents on sustainable timber and nontimber off-take, value of carbon sequestration, and local (and potentially global) willingness to pay for the external services that forests provide.

Chapter 2

The Wealth Stock Estimates

What constitutes wealth? Traditionally attention has been focused on produced capital such as buildings, machinery, equipment, and infrastructure. The wealth estimates introduced below extend these measures by accounting for exhaustible resources, renewable resources, and agricultural land. The estimates also include *intangible* capital, which encompasses raw labor, human capital (the stock of human skills and know-how), social capital, and the quality of institutions.

Economic theory tells us that there is a strong link between changes in wealth and the sustainability of development—if a country (or a household, for that matter) is running down its assets, it is not on a sustainable path. For the link to hold, however, the notion of wealth must be truly comprehensive. This is a major motivation for expanding the measure of wealth.

We are also interested in several basic questions concerning the wealth of nations:

- What is the most important component of wealth across countries?
- How do the shares of different types of wealth vary with income? Does the value of natural wealth increase or decrease as countries develop?

These and other questions are examined below.

This chapter presents wealth stock estimates for 120 developing and developed countries for the year 2000. The details of the wealth estimation procedure and country-level data can be found in Appendixes 1 and 2.

The Richest and the Poorest

Aggregate wealth estimates are presented in tables 2.1 and 2.2, which highlight the 10 wealthiest and poorest countries. The results are hardly surprising. Switzerland heads a list in which the top performers are all Organization for Economic Co-operation and Development (OECD) countries. European countries—two in Scandinavia—dominate the list along with the United States and Japan. The composition of wealth is very consistent across these countries, with the exception of Norway and Japan. Norway's natural capital, which includes oil and gas resources from the North Sea, accounts for 12 percent of total wealth. Japan stands out for its large share of produced capital—30 percent of the total.

The list of the 10 poorest countries is presented in table 2.2. If Europe heads the top-10 list, Sub-Saharan Africa dominates the bottom-10 list. Countries in table 2.2 are characterized by high levels of natural capital—at least 25 percent of the total. Ethiopia has the lowest level of total wealth, combined with a very low share of produced capital. A similar pattern can be observed in Burundi, Niger, Chad, and Madagascar. Nepal is the only country in the table that is not in Sub-Saharan Africa.

Table 2.1 Total Wealth: Top-10 Countries, 2000

Country (descending order of per capita wealth)	Wealth per capita ($)	Natural capital (%)	Produced capital (%)	Intangible capital (%)
Switzerland	648,241	1	15	84
Denmark	575,138	2	14	84
Sweden	513,424	2	11	87
United States	512,612	3	16	82
Germany	496,447	1	14	85
Japan	493,241	0	30	69
Austria	493,080	1	15	84
Norway	473,708	12	25	63
France	468,024	1	12	86
Belgium-Luxembourg	451,714	1	13	86

Source: Authors.

Table 2.2 Total Wealth: Bottom-10 Countries, 2000

Country (descending order of per capita wealth)	Wealth per capita ($)	Natural capital (%)	Produced capital (%)	Intangible capital (%)
Madagascar	5,020	33	8	59
Chad	4,458	42	6	52
Mozambique	4,232	25	11	64
Guinea-Bissau	3,974	47	14	39
Nepal	3,802	32	16	52
Niger	3,695	53	8	39
Congo, Rep. of	3,516	265	180	–346
Burundi	2,859	42	7	50
Nigeria	2,748	147	24	–71
Ethiopia	1,965	41	9	50

Source: Authors.

Intangible capital appears with a negative sign in some instances, which is an empirical possibility given that it is calculated as a residual—the difference between total wealth and the sum of natural and produced resources. Box 2.1 explores what it means to have a negative intangible capital residual.

The Architecture of the Wealth Estimates

Measuring capital stocks is a complex task. Capital can be valued using two basic methods:

- It can be valued as the sum of the additions, minus the subtractions, made over time to an initial stock—summing up the value of gross investments and subtracting depreciation of produced capital, for example.
- Alternatively, capital can be valued as the net present value (NPV) of the income it is able to produce over time. This is what an investor would be willing to pay for a capital good.

As a practical matter we employ the first method, also called the *perpetual inventory method* (PIM), to estimate the value of produced capital stocks,

Figure 2.1 Estimating the Components of Wealth

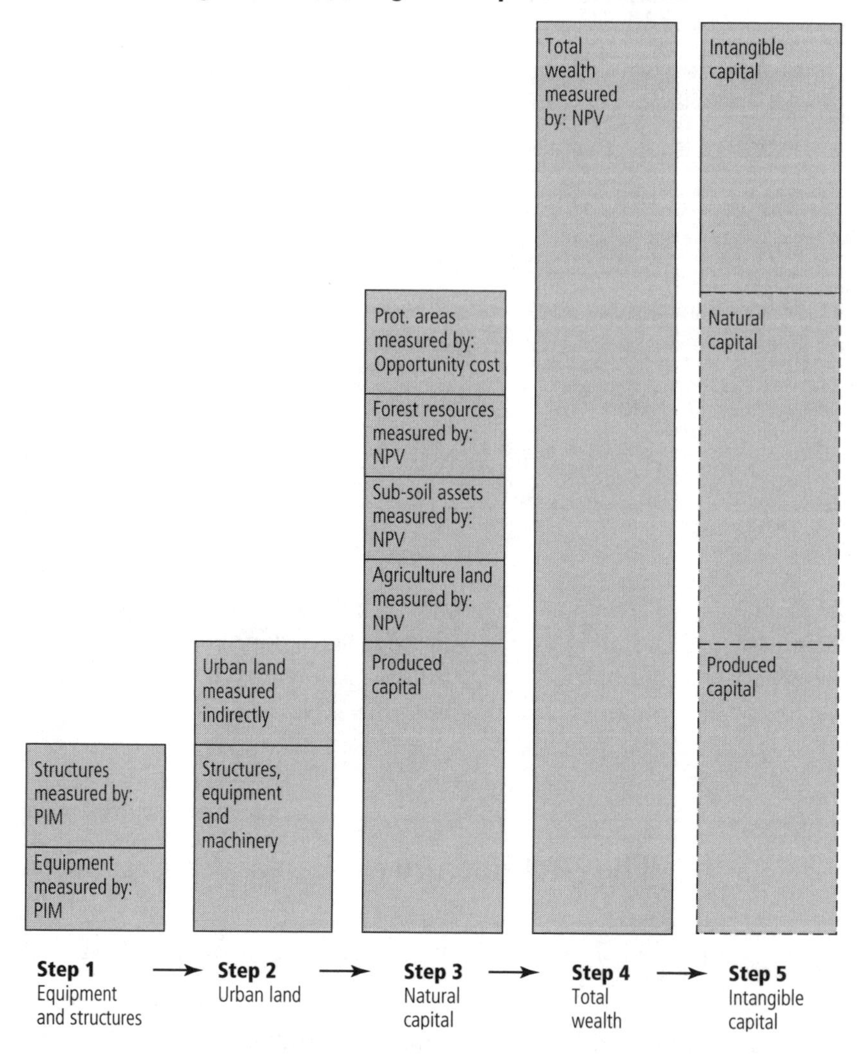

while the second method is used to value stocks of natural resources. Figure 2.1 represents the steps in estimating wealth components.

Produced capital is the sum of machinery, equipment, and structures (including infrastructure). Urban land is not considered to be a natural resource, and so is lumped in with produced capital in the wealth estimates. The value of urban land is calculated as a percentage of the value of machinery, equipment, and structures.

Natural capital is the sum of nonrenewable resources (including oil, natural gas, coal, and mineral resources), cropland, pastureland, forested areas (including areas used for timber extraction and nontimber forest products), and protected areas. The values for nontimber forest resources and protected areas are estimated only crudely. In the case of nontimber forest products, world average values of benefits per hectare, distinguishing developed and developing countries, are applied to a share of the country's forested area (values are derived from Lampietti and Dixon 1995). Protected areas are valued using country-specific per-hectare values for cropland or pastureland (whichever is lower). This severely undervalues the Serengeti Plain, for example, but possibly overvalues some of the Arctic parks.

As noted above, most natural resources are valued by taking the present value of resource rents—the economic profit on exploitation—over an assumed lifetime. While forests can, in principle, yield benefits forever if sustainably managed, we account for overexploitation by calculating the effective lifetime of the resource given current harvest rates.

The next step is the measurement of total wealth. Measuring total wealth as the sum of its components makes intuitive sense, but this is limited by data and methodological constraints. We have few good tools for valuing human capital, for example, and even fewer for valuing social or institutional capital. In other cases, such as fisheries, we simply lack data. The alternative is to rely on economic theory, which defines total wealth as the net present value of future consumption. We therefore measure total wealth by assuming a future consumption stream and calculating the net present value in year 2000. However, some countries have unsustainable levels of consumption, which is signaled by negative net or genuine saving levels (see chapter 3). In these cases consumption is decreased by the amount of negative saving in order to arrive at a sustainable level of consumption.

Intangible capital is calculated as a residual, the difference between total wealth and the sum of produced and natural capital. Since it includes all assets that are neither natural nor produced, the residual necessarily includes human capital—the sum of knowledge, skills, and know-how possessed by the population. It also includes the institutional infrastructure of the country as well as the social capital—the level of trust among people in a society and their ability to work together toward common goals. Finally, the residual includes net foreign financial assets through the returns generated by these assets. For example, if a country is a debtor, then interest payments on the foreign debt depress consumption, reducing total wealth and therefore the intangible residual.

A special caveat applies to natural capital. While the wealth estimates include a large number of assets, the exercise is far from perfect. Assets for which data are lacking include subsoil water, diamonds, and fisheries. To the extent that countries profit from these resources, their value is implicitly included in the total wealth aggregate and, hence, ends up in the intangible capital residual.

The services provided by ecosystems, such as the hydrological functions of forests and the pollination services of insects and birds, are indirectly captured in the natural wealth estimates through the values of cropland and pastureland, but no explicit value for ecosystem services is estimated, owing to data limitations. Figure 2.2 summarizes what is captured and what is not in the wealth estimates.

Figure 2.2 The Inclusion of Environment and Natural Resources in the Wealth Estimates

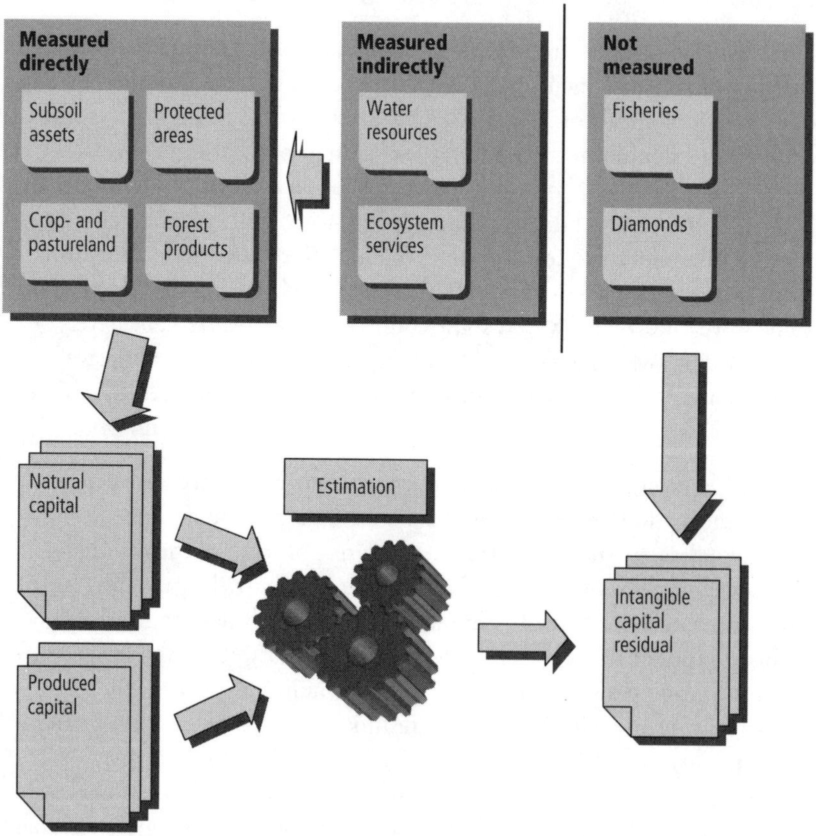

The lack of data on fisheries may be particularly important in a number of countries. Food and Agriculture Organization of the United Nations (FAO) figures show that the roughly 90 million tons of captured fish have a landed value of $78 billion annually. The export value of the total world trade of fish and fisheries products (including aquaculture) was $58.2 billion in 2002. Half of this value comes from developing countries, many of which also generate substantial additional income from licensing foreign access to their fisheries.

Similarly, missing data on diamonds has a serious impact on the wealth accounts of countries such as Botswana. Lange and others (2003) report diamond wealth of $7,400 per capita in Botswana in 1997. This would increase Botswana's value of natural capital to roughly $10,600 per person (25 percent of the total), and reduce intangible capital to about $21,000 (52 percent of the total).

Since many wealth components are estimated as a net present value of a flow of benefits, the calculations require assumptions regarding the time horizon and the discount rate. Throughout the calculations, we assumed a time horizon of 25 years, which coincides roughly with a human generation. So, for example, total wealth is calculated as the net present value of sustainable consumption from the year 2000 to 2025. With respect to discounting, since the focus is on sustainable development, the discount rate used is the one a government would choose in allocating resources across generations. This is an argument in favor of using a social discount rate instead of a private discount rate. Estimates of the Social Rate of Return on Investment (SRRI—another name for the social discount rate) for industrialized countries report values between 2 and 4 percent (Pearce and Ulph 1999). We assume an SRRI at the upper limit, 4 percent. This would likely be too low for fast-growing economies such as China, while being high for slow-growing economies in Sub-Saharan Africa. We choose a single discount rate for all countries in order to facilitate comparisons.

What the Data Reveal

Having explained the methods and caveats in the estimation of wealth, the remainder of the chapter is devoted to an overview of the wealth estimates. Subsequent chapters deal with specific aspects and go deeper into the

Table 2.3 Wealth per Capita by Region and Income Group, 2000

	$ per capita				% share of total wealth		
Region	Total wealth	Natural capital	Produced capital	Intangible capital	Natural capital	Produced capital	Intangible capital
Latin America and the Caribbean	67,955	8,059	10,830	49,066	12	16	72
Sub-Saharan Africa	10,730	2,535	1,449	6,746	24	13	63
South Asia	6,906	1,749	1,115	4,043	25	16	59
East Asia and the Pacific	11,958	2,511	3,189	6,258	21	27	52
Middle East and North Africa	22,186	7,989	4,448	9,749	36	20	44
Europe and Central Asia	40,209	11,031	12,299	16,880	27	31	42
Income group							
Low-income countries	7,216	2,075	1,150	3,991	29	16	55
Lower-middle-income countries	23,612	4,398	4,962	14,253	19	21	60
Upper-middle-income countries	72,897	10,921	16,481	45,495	15	23	62
High-income OECD countries	439,063	9,531	76,193	353,339	2	17	80
World	90,210	4,681	16,160	69,369	5	18	77

Source: Authors.
Note: The data in this table include oil-exporting countries.

analysis. The discussion here is focused on the estimates aggregated by region and income group, while appendix 2 provides the country-level estimates.

Table 2.3 summarizes total wealth by region and income group. Worldwide, natural capital accounts for 5 percent of total wealth, produced capital for 18 percent, and intangible capital 77 percent. The average world citizen has a total wealth of $90,000, an amount similar to the per capita wealth of Brazil ($87,000), Libya ($89,000), or Croatia ($91,000). Most of this wealth is in the form of intangible capital. Tangible assets include produced capital, totaling $16,000, and natural capital, $5,000. Natural capital is dominated by land resources (cropland, pastureland, and protected areas), which constitute 51 percent of total natural resources (see table 2.4, where natural wealth is broken down into its components). Subsoil assets account for 41 percent, and timber and nontimber forest resources account for the remaining 8 percent of natural capital.

Table 2.4 The Composition of Natural Capital by Region and Income Group, 2000

Region	Natural capital	Subsoil assets	Timber resources	NTFR	PA	Cropland	Pastureland
Latin America and the Caribbean	8,059	3,845 48%	359 4%	424 5%	411 5%	1,942 24%	1,077 13%
Sub-Saharan Africa	2,535	979 39%	225 9%	129 5%	64 3%	925 36%	213 8%
South Asia	1,749	189 11%	53 3%	13 1%	109 6%	1,183 68%	202 12%
East Asia and the Pacific	2,511	710 28%	140 6%	43 2%	79 3%	1,415 56%	125 5%
Middle East and North Africa	7,989	6,002 75%	14 0%	14 0%	58 1%	1,510 19%	390 5%
Europe and Central Asia	11,031	6,532 59%	225 2%	688 6%	779 7%	1,622 15%	1,185 11%
Income group							
Low-Income countries	2,075	487 23%	119 6%	49 2%	104 5%	1,134 55%	182 9%
Lower-middle-income countries	4,398	1,933 44%	159 4%	182 4%	189 4%	1,526 35%	409 9%
Upper-middle-income countries	10,921	7,031 64%	265 2%	206 2%	463 4%	1,872 17%	1,084 10%
High-income OECD countries	9,531	3,825 40%	747 8%	183 2%	1,215 13%	2,008 21%	1,552 16%
World	4,681	1,933 41%	247 5%	134 3%	343 7%	1,477 32%	547 12%

Source: Authors.
Note: The data in this table include oil-exporting countries. NTFR: Nontimber forest resources. PA: Protected areas. Figures are in dollars per capita and in percents.

Of course, using world averages obscures important differences. The level of total wealth per capita and the distribution of different types of wealth vary hugely across regions and income groups.

Table 2.4 shows that endowments of natural capital vary substantially across regions of the world. Subsoil assets abound in the Middle East and North Africa, Europe and Central Asia, and Latin America and the Caribbean. Agricultural land (cropland plus pastureland) has a relatively high importance in East Asia and the Pacific, South Asia, and Sub-Saharan Africa.

From this broad analysis of the wealth estimates a few stylized facts emerge.

Intangible Capital Is the Largest Share of Total Wealth

The most striking aspect of the wealth estimates is the high values for intangible capital. Nearly 85 percent of the countries in our sample have an intangible capital share of total wealth greater than 50 percent. This outcome validates the classical economists' intuition that human capital and other intangibles play a major role in economic development. Intangible capital varies widely across income groups and across regions. In the developing world, the Latin America and the Caribbean region has the highest level of intangible capital, $49,000 per capita. The lowest levels are in South Asia, $4,000 per capita, and Sub-Saharan Africa, less than $7,000 per capita.

Chapter 7 uses a production function framework to divide the intangible capital residual into the components that explain its variation across countries. Human capital (measured through years of schooling) and governance (measured through a rule of law index) together explain nearly 90 percent of the variation in intangible capital.

Intangible capital comprises 80 percent of the total wealth in high-income countries. It is close to zero, and often negative, in major oil exporters such as Nigeria, Algeria, and Venezuela. What is special about oil states? Box 2.1 analyzes this issue.

Box 2.1 Why a Negative Level of Intangible Capital

As seen in table 2.2 in appendix 2, a number of countries appear to have negative levels of intangible capital. This is the case for the Republic of Congo, Nigeria, Algeria, the Syrian Arab Republic, and Gabon. Although positive, very low levels of intangible capital are estimated for República Bolivariana de Venezuela, Moldova, Guyana, and the Russian Federation (see table on the next page).

A negative level of intangible capital is possible by construction because it is calculated as a residual—the difference between total wealth (the present value of future consumption) and the sum of produced and natural capital. The real question is how to interpret a negative or extremely low value of intangible capital.

Intangible Capital and the Composition of Wealth in Highly Resource-Dependent Countries

		Percentage share of total wealth		
Country	Intangible capital per capita ($)	Natural capital	Produced capital	Intangible capital
Russian Federation	6,029	44	40	16
Guyana	2,176	65	21	14
Moldova	1,173	37	49	13
Venezuela, R. B. de	4,360	60	30	10
Gabon	−3,215	66	41	−7
Syrian Arab Rep.	−1,598	84	32	−15
Algeria	−3,418	71	47	−18
Nigeria	−1,959	147	24	−71
Congo, Rep. of	−12,158	265	180	−346

Source: Authors.

Recall that total wealth is the present value of *sustainable* consumption. What the low and negative values of intangible capital are really saying is that the level of GNI is *too low* in these countries. If it were higher, then higher levels of consumption per capita could be sustained and both total wealth and intangible wealth would be higher. GNI is too low in these countries in the sense that they are achieving extremely low rates of return on their produced, human, and institutional capital. This is a classic symptom of the *resource curse* as documented by Auty (2001) and Gylfason (2001).

Lower Shares but Higher Levels of Natural Capital in Richer Countries

High-income countries have a relatively low ratio of natural resources to total assets compared with poorer countries. Is income in poorer countries constrained by a high level of natural-resource dependence? Without further analysis it is not possible to draw a general conclusion regarding the causal link between asset composition and income. The fact that lower-income countries are more dependent on natural resources than their richer peers seems to be an intrinsic feature of the development process.

While rich countries clearly were more heavily forested and had more abundant wildlife and fish resources in the past, it is striking that the value of natural capital per person is higher today in high-income countries than in low- and middle-income countries. In high-income countries it is likely that preferences linked to higher incomes are playing a key role in fostering more careful management of natural capital, while higher levels of other forms of capital may interact positively with the value of natural capital—specialized knowledge and greater mechanization, for example, boosts the yields on cropland in rich countries compared with the yields in poor countries.

Poorer Countries Rely on Land Resources

Given the importance of natural capital in the wealth of poor countries, the individual subcomponents merit consideration. Excluding large oil-exporting countries, land resources are very important in low-income countries, with a 75 percent share of natural wealth (69 percent consisting of cropland and pastureland), followed by subsoil assets at 17 percent. By comparison, in middle-income countries land resources account for 61 percent of natural capital, while subsoil assets account for 31 percent. Figure 2.3 summarizes these findings.

The importance of land resources (cropland, pastureland, and protected areas) decreases with the level of income. This suggests a potential poverty-land-dependence trap in low-income countries. Countries in which land resources account for more than one third of total wealth, such as Niger, Burundi, and Moldova, all belong to the low-income country group.

By contrast, low-income countries, as a group, are not particularly dependent on subsoil assets. Countries rich in mineral and energy resources may be found in each of the income groups.

Figure 2.3 The Composition of Natural Capital (High Oil Exporters Excluded)

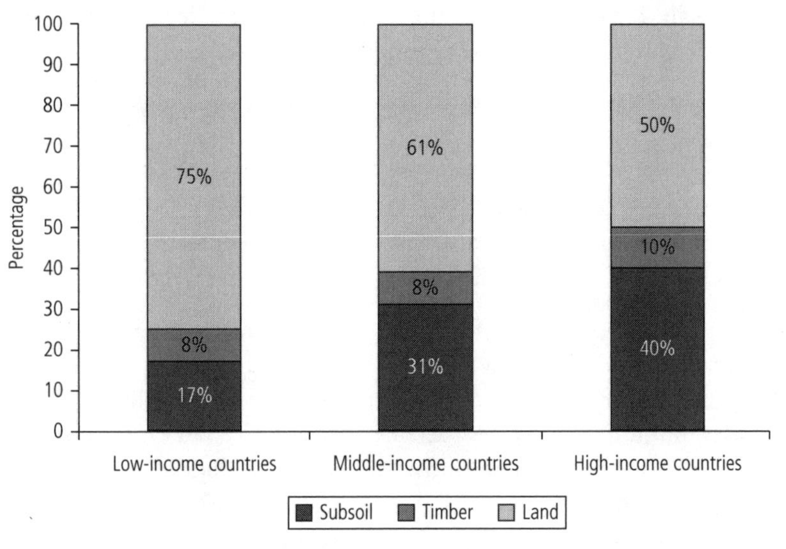

Source: Authors.

Key Conclusions on Wealth

The ranking of countries by total wealth per capita in appendix 2 does not differ hugely from the ranking by gross domestic product (GDP) per capita. It would be surprising if it did, since GDP is the return on total wealth. There are important exceptions to this, particularly the highly resource-dependent economies featured in box 2.1. But the primary interest in measuring wealth is not to rank countries. It is to better understand the composition of wealth and how this composition varies across levels of income.

The main conclusions from the wealth analysis include:

- Low-income countries are highly dependent on natural resources. The share of natural capital is greater than the share of produced capital in these countries.
- Cropland and pastureland is the largest share, nearly 70 percent, of natural wealth in poor countries (excluding oil exporters).

- Overall, intangible capital is the preponderant share of wealth in virtually all countries, with the share increasing with income. The particularly inefficient use of produced and intangible assets in the most resource-dependent economies leads to the anomalous result of apparently negative shares of intangible capital in these economies.
- The level of natural wealth per capita actually rises with income. This contradicts the common assumption, that development necessarily entails the depletion of the environment and natural resources.

The declining *share* of natural wealth as income increases is not an argument that natural resources are somehow unimportant—food, fiber, timber, minerals, and energy are all plainly needed to sustain lives and economies, but it does indicate a decline in relative importance. The key point is that low-income countries are highly dependent on natural resources *now*. How these resources are managed will affect both current welfare and the prospects for development in poor countries.

PART 2

CHANGES IN WEALTH

Chapter 3

Recent Genuine Saving Estimates

However sustainable development is defined,[1] achieving it is, at heart, the process of maintaining wealth for future generations. Wealth is conceived broadly to include not only the traditional measures of capital, such as produced and human capital, but also natural assets. Natural capital comprises assets such as land, forests, and subsoil resources. All three types of capital—produced, human, and natural—are key inputs to sustaining economic growth.

The standard national accounts measure the change in a country's wealth by focusing solely on produced assets. A country's provision for the future is measured by its gross national saving, which represents the total amount of produced output that is not consumed. Gross national saving, however, can say little about sustainable development, since assets depreciate over time. Net national saving equals gross national saving minus depreciation of fixed capital and is one step closer to measuring sustainability. The next step in measuring sustainability is to adjust net saving for the accumulation of other assets—human capital, the environment, and natural resources—that underpin development.

This chapter introduces the concept of *genuine* saving (formally known as adjusted net saving) first derived in Pearce and Atkinson (1993) and Hamilton (1994). It then presents and discusses the empirical calculations of genuine saving rates available for over 140 countries (tabulated in appendix 3). Genuine saving provides a much broader indicator of sustainability by valuing changes in natural resources, environmental quality, and human capital, in addition to the traditional measure of changes in produced assets provided by net saving.

Negative genuine saving rates imply that total wealth is in decline; policies leading to persistently negative genuine saving are unsustainable. In addition to serving as an indicator of sustainability, genuine saving has the advantage of presenting resource and environmental issues within a framework that finance and development planning ministries can understand. It makes the growth-environment trade-off explicit, since those countries pursuing economic growth today, at the expense of natural resources, will be notable by their depressed rates of genuine saving. Of the 140 countries where genuine saving is estimated for 2003, just over 30 have negative saving rates.

Calculating Genuine Saving

Figure 3.1 provides a flow chart describing each of the main steps in the genuine saving calculation. Starting at the top of figure 3.1, the calculation of genuine saving begins with gross national saving. Gross national saving is calculated as the difference between the gross national income (GNI) and public and private consumption plus net current transfers. From this the consumption of fixed capital is subtracted, giving the traditional measure of net national saving. Consumption of fixed capital represents the replacement value of capital used up in the process of production.

In the traditional measure of net national saving only that portion of total expenditure on education that goes toward fixed capital (such as school buildings) is included as a part of saving; the rest is treated as consumption. From the perspective of broadening the measure of wealth this is clearly unsatisfactory. Therefore, as a crude approximation, current operating expenditures on education, including wages and salaries and excluding capital investments in buildings and equipment, are added to net national saving.[2]

Natural resource depletion is then subtracted. The value of resource depletion is calculated as the total rents on resource extraction and harvest, where rents are estimated as the difference between the value of production at world prices and total costs of production, including depreciation of fixed capital and return on capital. The energy resources include oil, natural gas, and coal, while metals and minerals include bauxite, copper, gold, iron ore, lead, nickel, phosphate, silver, tin, and zinc.

Figure 3.1 Flow Chart of Genuine Saving Calculation

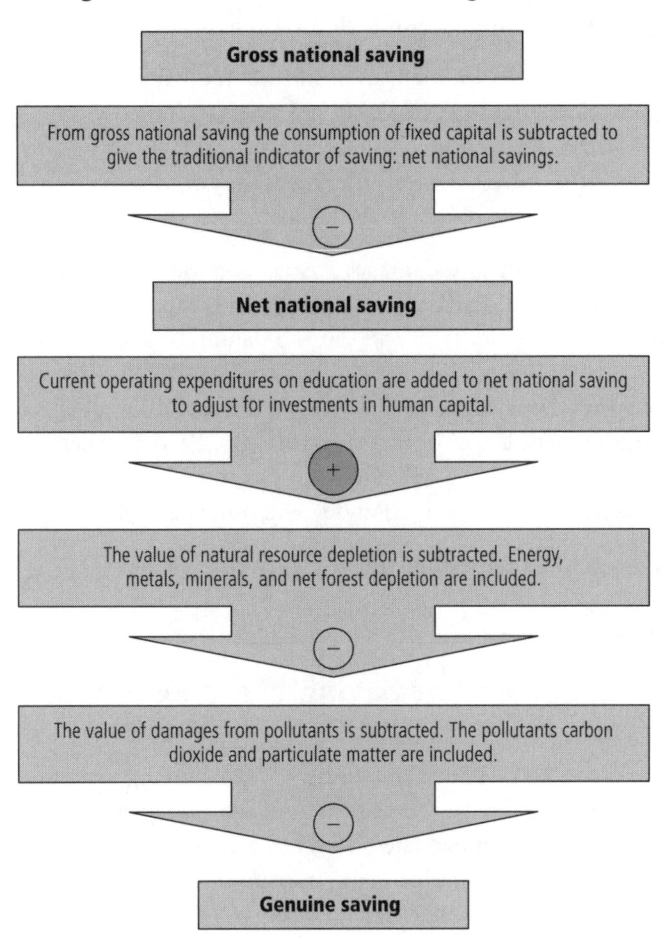

As a living resource, forest resources are fundamentally different from energy, metals, and minerals. The correction to the net saving rate is thus not simply rent on timber extraction, but rather rent on that portion of timber extraction that exceeds natural growth. If growth exceeds harvest, this figure is set to zero.

The genuine saving calculation also includes the value of damages from air pollution. Pollution damages can enter the national accounts in several ways. While, in theory, pollution damage to produced assets is included in depreciation figures, in practice, most statistical systems are not detailed enough to capture this. For example, acid rain damages to building materials are rarely fully accounted. The effects of pollution on output—damage to crops, for example—are already included in the standard national accounts, although not explicitly.

Next is the adjustment for damages from carbon dioxide, using a figure for marginal global damages of $20 (1995 prices) per metric ton of carbon emitted (Fankhauser 1994).[3] This represents the present value of marginal damages to crops, infrastructure, and human health over the time that emitted carbon dioxide resides in the atmosphere—over 100 years.

Finally, the value of health damages arising from particulate matter pollution is deducted. Particulate air pollution is capable of penetrating deep into the respiratory tract and causing damage, including premature mortality. The population-weighted average level of PM_{10} (particulate matter less than 10 microns in diameter) is estimated for all cities in each country with a population in excess of 100,000. Particulate emission damage is calculated as the willingness to pay to reduce the risk of mortality attributable to PM_{10} (Pandey and others 2005).

The net result of all these adjustments is genuine saving.

Interpreting Genuine Saving Estimates

Welfare can be sustained indefinitely if gross saving just equals the sum of depreciation of produced assets, depletion of natural resources, and pollution damages. This is the well-known Hartwick rule. A persistently negative genuine saving rate implies that a country is on an unsustainable path and welfare must fall in the future.

However, we should be cautious in interpreting a positive genuine saving rate. There are some important assets omitted from the analysis for methodological and empirical reasons, which may mean that saving rates are only apparently positive. First, fisheries can be a significant resource for a local or national economy. However, it can be very difficult to measure fish stocks and to attribute ownership to one country, not least because of their mobility. Soil erosion is another important issue, especially in agrarian economies. Attaching a value to soil erosion requires detailed local data that are not widely available, and it can be extremely difficult to disentangle the economic costs of soil erosion from the physical losses (see box 3.1). Diamonds are another important resource for some countries, most significantly in Angola, Botswana, the Democratic Republic of Congo, Namibia, the Russian Federation, and

South Africa. Diamonds are excluded from the analysis because of data availability issues and the lack of free-market prices.

Box 3.1 Soil Degradation and Changes in Wealth

Ideally, adjusted net or genuine saving should include the depletion and degradation of land resources, which contribute 18 percent of total wealth in low-income countries. However, data comparability and availability do not allow for systematic inclusion of this item in the saving analysis.

For many low-income countries that depend on the natural resource base for their development, the loss of soil quality can be a major problem. The UN Convention to Combat Desertification is a policy response to this trend, and the recently published *Millennium Ecosystem Assessment* (2005) points to land degradation in drylands, in particular in Africa and Central Asia, as one of the major challenges now facing the international community. Many of the poorest countries in the world face serious land degradation problems.

Statistical information on the cost of land degradation is not widely available, largely because the effects of erosion are complex to measure with accuracy. It is not sufficient to measure on-farm effects since the external consequences of erosion can be significant. Negative off-farm effects of erosion include siltation of dams, salinization, and loss of biodiversity. But there are also positive effects of erosion—for example, delta landscapes, such as the Nile Delta and Bangladesh, depend on the yearly deposit of soil and nutrients transported by rivers for their fertility.

It is probably safe to assume that soil erosion that goes considerably beyond natural levels has negative economic effects. Through case studies undertaken for seven developing countries in Africa, Asia, and Latin America it has been estimated that the problems of sustainable land management deduct 3 percent to 7 percent from agricultural GDP (Berry and others 2003). A study from Australia (Gretton and Salma 1996) estimates soil fertility loss equivalent to 6 percent of agricultural production. Soil losses can be significant.

The Genuine Saing Calculation: A Country Example

Figure 3.2 shows the steps in calculating genuine saving for Bolivia, one of the poorest countries in Latin America, with GDP per capita below $1,000. Bolivia is endowed with a wealth of natural resources, including minerals, oil, and huge deposits of natural gas discovered at the end of the 1990s.

Figure 3.2 Adjustments in the Genuine Saving Calculation for Bolivia (2003)

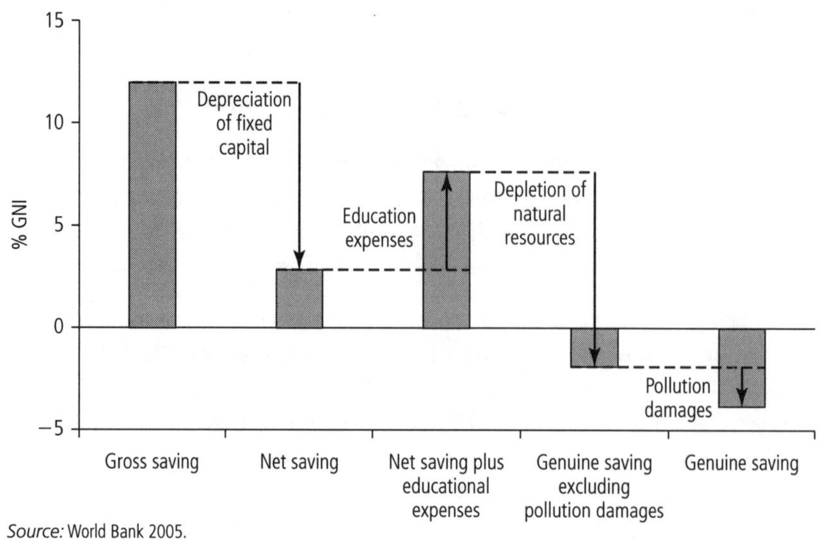

Source: World Bank 2005.

The first column in figure 3.2 shows the traditional measure of gross national saving in Bolivia, 12 percent of gross national income (GNI) in 2003. Deducting the depreciation of produced capital reveals a much lower net saving rate, less than 3 percent. Investments in education are estimated to be around 5 percent of GNI, bringing the saving rate up to nearly 8 percent as shown by the third column in figure 3.2.

Following this, adjustments are made for depletion of natural resources. Resource rents from Bolivia's extraction of oil and gas are deducted, as well as the rents from gold, silver, lead, zinc, and tin. Depletion of energy, metals, and minerals amount to over 9 percent of the GNI. While deforestation is deemed to be a problem in Bolivia, available data suggest that net forest depletion is zero. As a result of these deductions for resource depletion, Bolivia's genuine saving rate is negative.

Finally, the deduction for pollution damages leads to a bottom-line estimate of Bolivia's genuine saving rate of minus 3.8 percent of GNI. Bolivia is currently on an unsustainable development path.

Regional Disparities

The calculation of aggregate genuine saving rates by region reveals some striking differences between regions of the world as shown

Figure 3.3 Genuine Saving Rates by Region

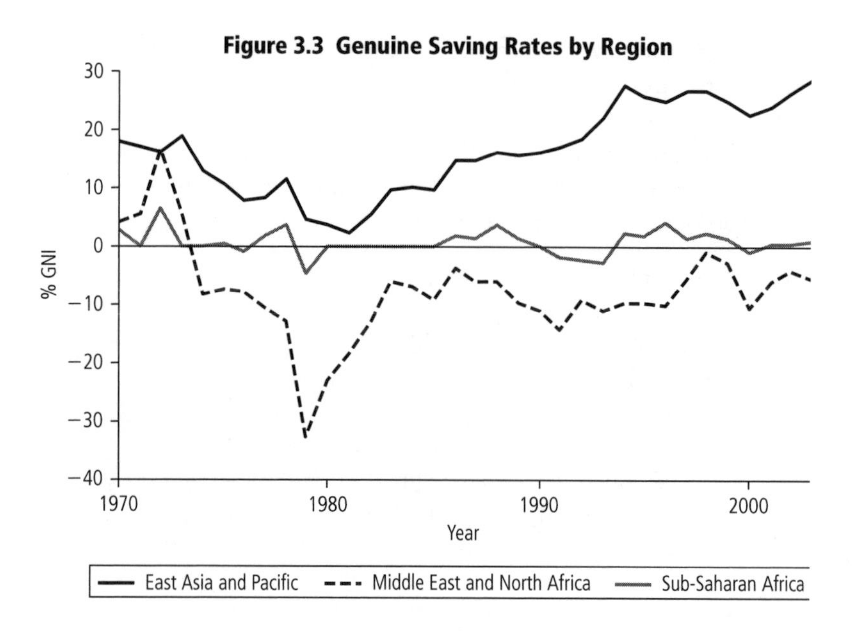

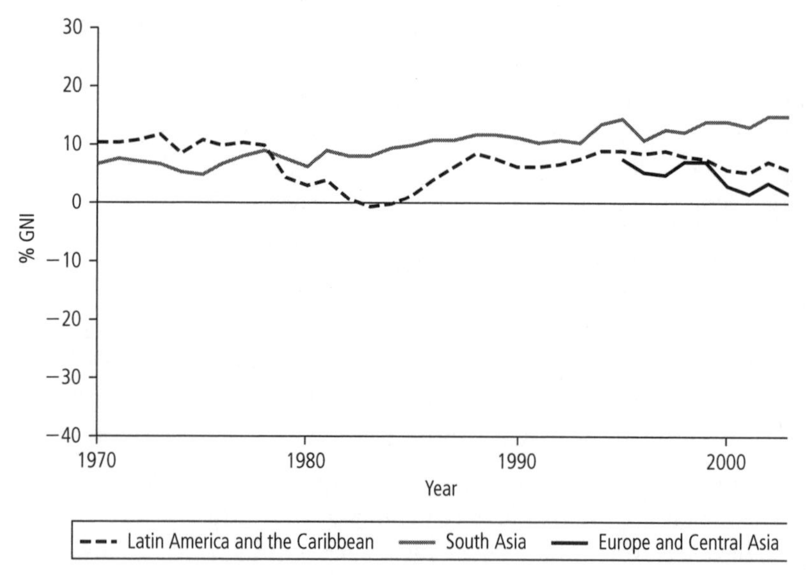

Source: World Bank 2005.

in figure 3.3. The Middle East and North Africa stands out for its consistently negative saving rate, reflecting high dependence on petroleum extraction. However, not all countries in the region have negative genuine saving rates. Jordan, Morocco, and Tunisia had consistently positive genuine saving rates over the period, exceeding 15 percent of GNI.

Regional genuine saving rates are highly sensitive to changes in world oil prices. The Iranian revolution from 1978 to 1979 followed by the Iran-Iraq war in 1980 resulted in crude oil prices more than doubling from $14 in 1978 to $35 per barrel in 1981. This is clearly shown in figure 3.3—genuine saving rates dipped in the region, largely owing to the consumption of sharply increased oil rents.

In stark contrast to the Middle East and North Africa stands the East Asia and Pacific region, with recent aggregate genuine saving figures nearing 30 percent, driven largely by China. This diverse region has enjoyed steady economic growth and progress toward poverty reduction. From 1999 to 2004, the number of East Asians living on less than $2 a day fell from 50 to 34 percent, or by about 250 million people. The boom in economic performance from the second half of the 1980s until the Asian financial crisis in 1997 is reflected in the genuine saving numbers, largely driven by increases in gross national saving.

In Sub-Saharan Africa, the poorest region in the world, the number of people living in extreme poverty has almost doubled, from 164 million in 1981 to 314 million today. Genuine saving rates in the region have been hovering around zero. The aggregation masks wide disparities between countries in the region. Positive genuine saving rates in countries such as Kenya, Tanzania, and South Africa are offset by strongly negative genuine saving rates in resource-dependent countries such as Nigeria and Angola, which have genuine saving rates of minus 30 percent.

South Asia displays consistently strong genuine saving rates. The regional aggregate genuine saving rate has been fluctuating between 10 and 15 percent since 1985, with India dominating the aggregate figure. Nepal is the region's new strong saver with genuine saving rates reaching nearly 30 percent in 2003. Nepal's gross national saving rate has been steadily increasing from the 1990s to the present day.

Latin American genuine saving rates have remained fairly constant throughout the 1990s. The large economies in the region, Mexico and Brazil, have positive genuine saving rates in excess of 5 percent. However, for the region's largest oil producer, República Bolivariana de Venezuela, saving rates tell a different story. Like many other oil producers, República Bolivariana de Venezuela's genuine saving rate has been persistently negative since the late 1970s.

Regional genuine saving data for Eastern Europe and Central Asia are only available from 1995. Saving rates have fallen from over

7.7 percent in 1995 to 1.7 percent in 2003. Of the 23 countries for which data were available in the region, 17 have positive genuine saving rates in 2003, averaging around 10 percent of GNI. However, the oil states of Azerbaijan, Kazakhstan, Uzbekistan, Turkmenistan, and the Russian Federation all have persistently negative genuine saving rates, thus pulling the regional aggregate downwards.

Consuming Resource Rents

Stocks of exhaustible resources such as oil represent a potential source of development finance. The question for countries with resource endowments is whether to consume these resource rents, providing current welfare but at a cost to future generations, or to invest the rents in other assets. Figure 3.4 scatters genuine saving rates against mineral and energy rents for resource-rich countries (defined as countries with exhaustible resource shares in excess of 1 percent of GNI).

Figure 3.4 shows that as resource rents increase as a percentage of GNI, genuine saving rates tend to decline. This implies that a significant proportion of natural resource rents are being consumed rather than

Figure 3.4 Genuine Saving and Exhaustible Resource Share (share 2003)

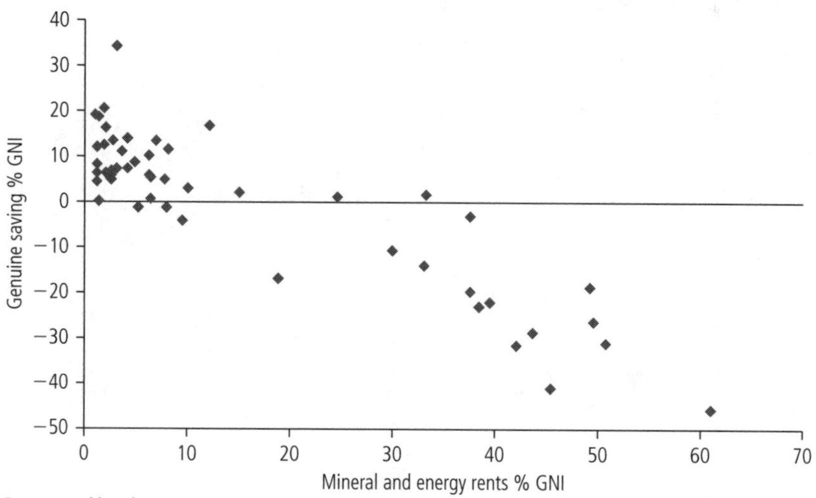

Source: World Bank 2005.

invested in other productive assets. Chapter 4 explores this issue further and finds that the consumption rather than investment of resource rents is common in resource-rich countries.

Income and Saving

Genuine saving estimates for the 1970s reveal a worrying trend: rich countries had considerably higher saving rates than poorer countries, implying a potentially wider divergence in income and wealth between high-income and low-income countries. In 1970, high-income countries were saving 15 percent more of their GNI than low-income countries. Genuine saving rates for low-income countries were positive in aggregate, but only equal to 4 percent of GNI. However, as shown in figure 3.5, genuine saving rates have converged over time. In fact, in 2003 high-income countries were saving less as a percentage of GNI than both low- and middle-income countries. High-income countries saving rates as a percentage of GNI have declined over time, while saving rates for low- and middle-income countries have increased.

Figure 3.5 Genuine Saving Rates by Income Group

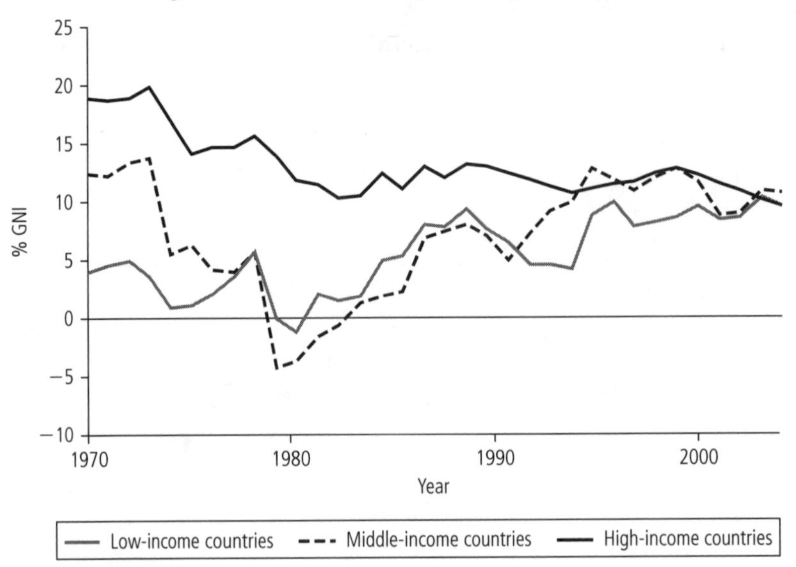

Source: World Bank 2005.

Saving and Growth

Figure 3.6 scatters genuine saving rates (as percentage of GDP) against GDP growth in 2003. Countries in the top-right quadrant have positive GDP growth rates and positive genuine saving rates. These economies are growing and, according to the genuine saving measure, not at the expense of future generations. This points to a positive future for countries like Botswana, China, and Ghana, all of whom have strong economic growth and positive genuine saving rates.

Countries in the top-left-hand quadrant of figure 3.6 are experiencing contracting economies with declining GDP. However, these countries have positive genuine saving rates, implying they are still investing for the future.

Traditional indicators of economic growth would suggest that those countries in the bottom-right-hand corner of figure 3.6 are doing well—economic growth is positive. However, when genuine saving is taken into consideration, this optimistic story changes. Countries such as Nigeria, Angola, Uzbekistan, and Azerbaijan all have growing economies, but negative genuine saving rates may be imperiling future generations.

Figure 3.6 Genuine Saving Rates against Economic Growth (2003)

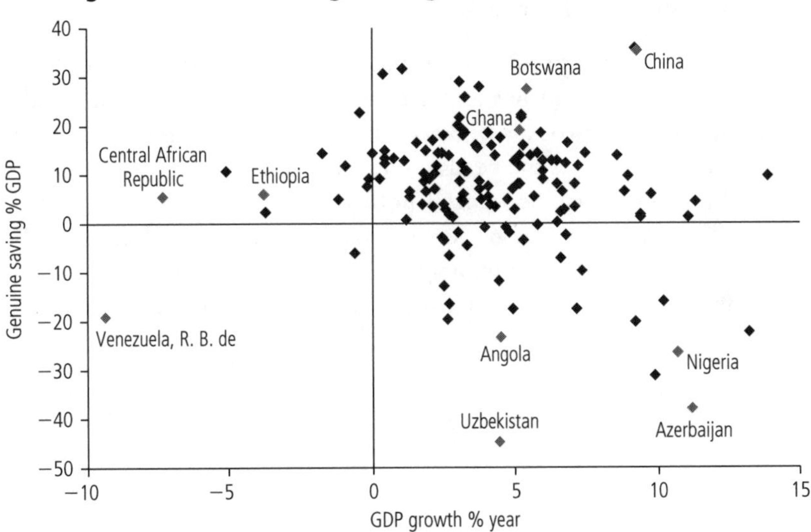

Source: World Bank 2005.

Countries in the bottom-left-hand quadrant face the biggest challenge. These economies are currently shrinking, while at the same time future welfare prospects are being reduced as a result of negative genuine saving rates. República Bolivariana de Venezuela is a case in point—persistent negative levels of economic growth[4] and genuine saving paint a troubling picture for future welfare.

Conclusions

Genuine saving provides an indicator of sustainability. There are many countries for which negative genuine saving rates are a reality (see appendix 3). In addition, those countries with low positive levels of genuine saving may also be pursuing a policy mix that will result in declining welfare over time, since measures of the depreciation of key assets may be masked by lack of data and methodological limitations.

Genuine saving rates differ widely throughout the world as shown by the regional aggregates in figure 3.3. The evidence suggests that while resource-rich countries have the potential to achieve sustainable development if resource rents are appropriately invested, many are not doing so, as shown in figure 3.4.

Genuine saving is useful to policy makers not only as an indicator of sustainability, but as a means of presenting resource and environmental issues within a framework familiar to finance and development planning ministries. It underlines the need to boost domestic saving, and hence, the need for sound macroeconomic policies, and it highlights the fiscal aspects of environment and resource management, since collecting resource royalties and charging pollution taxes are basic ways to both raise development finance and ensure efficient use of the environment.

Endnotes

1. See Pearce (1993) for a discussion on the definition of sustainable development.

2. For a further discussion of accounting for human capital in the genuine saving calculation see World Bank (1996).

3. Tol (2005) reviewed over 100 estimates of the marginal damage cost of carbon dioxide emissions. He found a large range of uncertainty: the median cost was found to be $14 per ton of carbon and the mean to be $93/tC. On balance the use of the Fankhauser (1994) estimate of $20/tC appears to be reasonable.

4. República Bolivariana de Venezuela GDP has declined by 11 percent between 1993 and 2003.

Chapter 4

The Importance of Investing Resource Rents: A Hartwick Rule Counterfactual

A substantial empirical literature documents the *resource curse* or *paradox of plenty*.[1] Resource-rich countries should enjoy an advantage in the development process, and yet these countries experienced lower GDP growth rates post-1970 than less well-endowed countries. A number of plausible explanations for this phenomenon have been suggested:

- Inflated currencies may impede the development of the nonoil export sector (this is known as "Dutch disease").
- Easy money in the form of resource rents may reduce incentives to implement needed economic reforms.
- Volatile resource prices may complicate macroeconomic management, exacerbating political conflicts over the sharing and management of resource revenues.

In the most extreme examples, levels of welfare in resource-rich countries are lower today than they were in 1970—development has not been sustained. The Hartwick rule (Hartwick 1977; Solow 1986) offers a rule-of-thumb for sustainability in exhaustible-resource economies—a constant level of consumption can be sustained if the value of investment equals the value of rents on extracted resources at each point in time. For countries dependent on such wasting assets, this rule offers a prescription for sustainable development, a prescription that Botswana, in particular, has followed with its diamond wealth (Lange and Wright 2004).

Drawing on a 30-year time series of resource rent data underlying chapter 3, this chapter constructs a Hartwick rule counterfactual: how rich would countries be in the year 2000 if they had followed the Hartwick rule since 1970? The empirical estimations below test two variants of the Hartwick rule—the standard rule, which amounts to keeping genuine saving precisely equal to zero at each point in time, and a version that assumes a constant level of positive genuine saving[2] at each point in time. The results, in many cases, are striking.

Hypothetical Estimates of Capital Stocks

The basic methodology for testing how rich countries would be if they had followed the Hartwick rule is to compare the estimates of produced capital stocks for the year 2000 derived in chapter 2 with the size these stocks could be if countries had followed the Hartwick rule or its variants since 1970. The approach is to accumulate resource rents starting from the base-year produced capital stock in 1970.

For simplicity, it is assumed that all resource rents are invested in produced capital, although theory suggests more generally that resource rents could be invested in a range of assets, including human capital and paying down of foreign debts. If any of the countries highlighted below had been investing their resource rents in human capital[3] or foreign assets (quite unlikely given the observed levels of per capita income and indebtedness), then the methodology would produce a biased picture of their investment performance. Furthermore, since the analysis is limited to investments in produced capital, we will refer to *genuine investment* rather than *genuine saving* in what follows.

In order to examine a variety of counterfactuals, four estimates of produced capital stock are derived using data covering 1970–2000:

- A baseline capital stock derived from investment series and a Perpetual Inventory Model (PIM)—this is the same stock reported in Chapter 2
- A capital stock derived from strict application of the standard Hartwick rule
- A capital stock derived from the constant genuine investment rule
- A capital stock derived from the maximum of observed net investment and the investment required under the constant genuine investment rule. All investment and resource rent series are measured in constant 1995 dollars at nominal exchange rates.

For genuine investment I^G, net investment N, depreciation of produced capital D, and resource depletion R, the following basic accounting identities hold at any point in time:

$$I^G \equiv I - D - R$$

$$N \equiv I - D = I^G + R$$

For constant genuine investment $\bar{I}^G$, we therefore estimate the counterfactual series of produced capital for each country as the sum of net investments:

$$K^*_{2000} = K_{1970} + \sum_{t=1971}^{2000} (\bar{I}^G + R_t)$$

$$K^{**}_{2000} = K_{1970} + \sum_{t=1971}^{2000} \max(N_t, \bar{I}^G + R_t)$$

Here K_{1970} is the baseline stock derived from the PIM. Two versions of K* are calculated in what follows—one with ${}_{V}*$ _ (the standard Hartwick rule), and a second with $\bar{I}^G$, equal to a constant 5 percent of 1987 GDP. The choice of a particular level of genuine investment for the analysis is arbitrary. We use 5 percent of 1987 GDP for the following reasons: there is some logic to choosing the midpoint of our time series of data from 1970 to 2000; 1987 is a slightly better choice, falling after the recession of the early 1980s, after the collapse of oil prices in 1986, and before the recession of the early 1990s; and a 5 percent genuine investment rate is roughly the average achieved by low-income countries over time.

Resource depletion is estimated as the sum of total rents on the extraction of the following commodities: crude oil, natural gas, coal, bauxite, copper, gold, iron, lead, nickel, phosphate, silver, and zinc. These data underlie the genuine saving estimates presented in chapter 3. While the underlying theory suggests that scarcity rents are what should be invested under the Hartwick rule (that is, price minus marginal extraction cost), the World Bank data do not include information on marginal extraction costs. This gives an upward bias to the hypothetical capital stock estimates under the genuine investment rules.

When comparing estimates of the stock of produced capital for different countries, it is worth noting that the PIM underestimates the capital stock for countries with very old infrastructures, as in most European countries. The value of roads, bridges, and buildings constructed many decades and even centuries ago is not captured by the PIM. Pritchett (2000) makes a different point, that low returns on investments imply that the PIM overestimates the value of capital in developing countries. Our methodology assumes that both the PIM and cumulated net investments are, in fact, adding up productive investments. To the extent that this is not the case, estimated capital stock levels should be lower in developing countries. But the primary interest here is to compare the level of actual capital in a given country with the counterfactual level of capital in the same country, had it followed a sustainability rule. This makes the point concerning relative investment efficiency across countries less salient.

Empirical Results

How rich would countries be in the year 2000 had they followed the Hartwick rule since 1970? Based on the preceding methodology, table A4.1 (see annex) presents the year 2000 produced capital stock and the changes in this stock, which would result from the alternative investment rules. The countries shown in this table are those having both exhaustible resources and a sufficiently long-time series of data on gross investment and resource rents. For reference, the table also shows the average share of resource rents in GDP from 1970 to 2000. Negative entries in this table imply that countries actually invested more than the policy rule would suggest.

For the standard Hartwick rule, figure 4.1 scatters resource dependence, expressed as the average share of exhaustible resource rents in GDP, against the percentage difference between actual capital accumulation and counterfactual capital accumulation. Using 5 percent of GDP as the threshold for high resource dependence, figure 4.1 divides countries into the four groups shown.

The top-right quadrant of the graph displays countries with high resource dependence and a counterfactual capital stock that is higher than the actual (baseline) capital stock. The bottom-left quadrant displays countries with low natural-resource dependence and baseline capital stock that is higher than would be obtained under the Hartwick rule. These

Figure 4.1 Resource Abundance and Capital Accumulation (standard Hartwick rule)

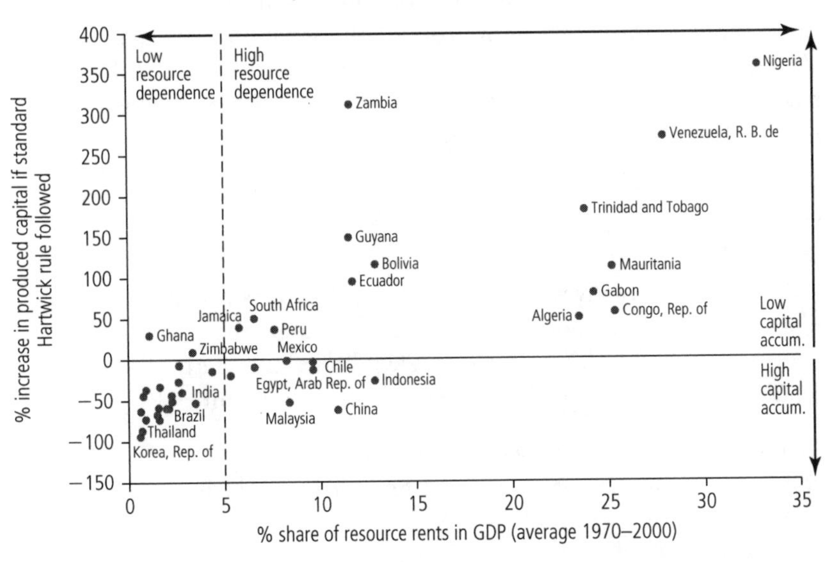

Source: Authors.

two quadrants include most of the countries in our sample, indicating a high negative correlation between resource abundance and the difference between baseline and counterfactual capital accumulation—a simple regression shows that a 1 percent increase in resource dependence is associated with a 9 percent increased difference between counterfactual and actual capital. Clearly the countries in the top-right quadrant have not been following the Hartwick rule. Economies with very low levels of capital accumulation, despite high rents, include Nigeria (oil), República Bolivariana de Venezuela (oil), Trinidad and Tobago (oil and gas), and Zambia (copper). With the exception of Trinidad and Tobago, all of these countries experienced declines in real per capita income from 1970 to 2000. In the opposite quadrant, economies with low exhaustible resource rent shares but high levels of capital accumulation include the Republic of Korea, Thailand, Brazil, and India. Some high-income countries are also in this group.

Figure 4.1 shows that no country with resource rents higher than 15 percent of GDP has followed the Hartwick rule. In many cases the differences are huge. Nigeria, a major oil exporter, could have had a year 2000 stock of produced capital five times higher than the actual stock. Moreover, if these investments had taken place, oil would play a much smaller role in the Nigerian economy today, with likely beneficial impacts on policies affecting other sectors of the economy. República Bolivariana de Venezuela could have four times as much produced capital. In per capita terms, the economies of Gabon, República Bolivariana de Venezuela, and Trinidad and Tobago, all rich in petroleum, could today have a stock of produced capital of roughly US$30,000 per person, comparable to the Republic of Korea (see figure 4.2).

Consumption, rather than investment, of resource rents is common in resource-rich countries, but there are exceptions to the trend. In the bottom-right quadrant of figure 4.1 are high resource-dependent countries that have invested more than the level of exhaustible resource rents. China, Egypt, Indonesia, and Malaysia stand out in this group, while Chile and Mexico have effectively followed the Hartwick rule—growth in produced capital is completely offset by resource depletion.

Among the countries with relatively low natural resource dependence and higher counterfactual capital, we find Ghana (gold and bauxite)

Figure 4.2 Actual and Counterfactual Produced Capital (per capita), 2000

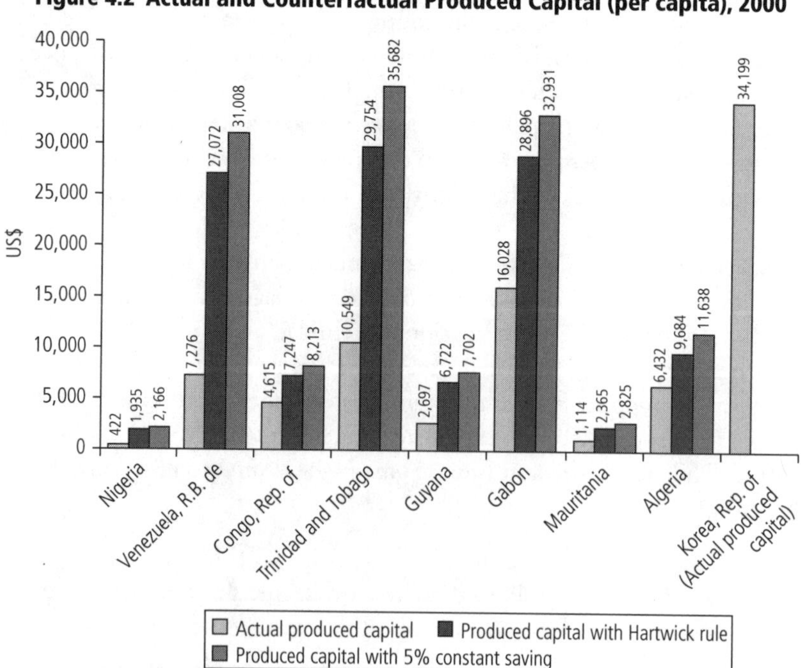

Source: Authors.
Note: 1995 dollars, nominal exchange rate.

and Zimbabwe (gold). This is indicative of very low levels of capital accumulation in these economies.

Figure 4.3 highlights countries which have invested more than their resource rents (as shown by the negative entries on the left side of the figure) but have failed to maintain constant genuine investment levels of at least 5 percent of 1987 GDP (as shown by the entries on the right). Developing countries in this group include Argentina, Cameroon, Cote d'Ivoire, and Madagascar. A number of high-income countries also appear in the figure. Sweden could have a stock of capital 36 percent higher if it had maintained constant genuine investment levels at the specified target. The corresponding difference for the United Kingdom is 27 percent, for Norway 25 percent, and for Denmark 22 percent.[4] The generally low level of genuine investment levels in the Nordic countries is particularly surprising. Are these countries trading off intergenerational equity against intragenerational equity? Further research would be required to clarify this, a question that is beyond the scope of this chapter.

Figure 4.3 Capital Accumulation under the Hartwick and Constant Net Investment Rules

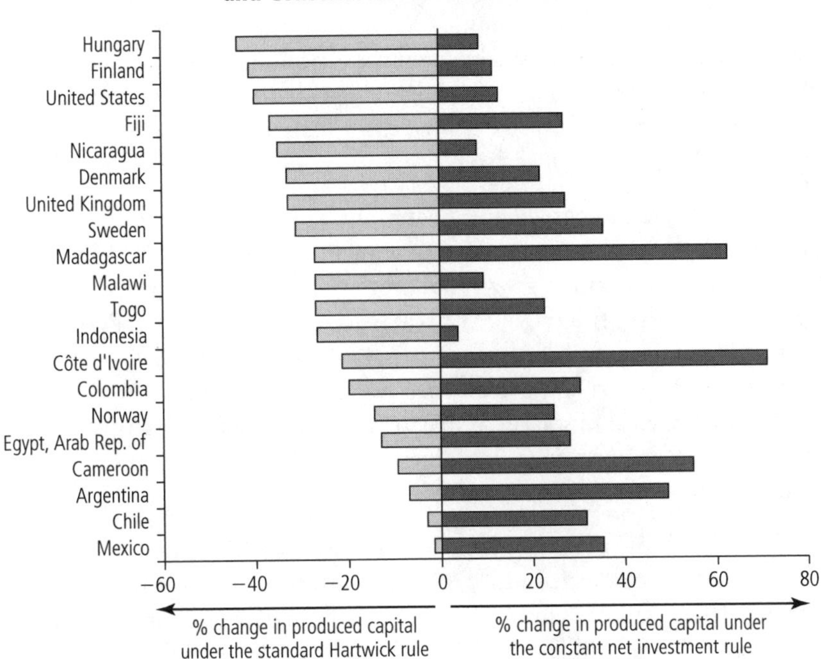

The next-to-last column in table A4.1 shows the change in produced assets for countries if they had genuine investments of at least 5 percent of 1987 GDP. The positive figures indicate that, with the exception of Singapore, all countries experienced at least one year from 1970 to 2000 where genuine investments were less than the prescribed constant level.

Conclusions

Applying the standard Hartwick rule as development policy would be extreme. It implies a commitment to zero net saving for all time. Conversely, the constant genuine saving rule embodies a commitment to building wealth at each point in time. In a risky world this may be a more palatable development policy.

The Hartwick rule counterfactual calculations show how even a moderate saving effort, equivalent to the average saving effort of the poorest countries in the world, could have substantially increased the wealth of resource-dependent economies. Of course, for the most resource-dependent countries such as Nigeria there is nothing moderate about the implied rate of investment. A Nigerian genuine investment rate of 36.1 percent of GDP in 1987 is what the calculations suggest under the constant genuine investment rule.

The saving rules presented here are appealing in their simplicity. Maintaining a constant level of genuine saving will yield a development path where consumption grows monotonically, even as exhaustible resource stocks are run down. The real world is more complex. Poor countries place a premium on maintaining consumption levels, with negative effects on saving—the alternative may be starvation. At the same time financial crises, social instability, and natural disasters all have deleterious effects on saving. Holding to a simple policy rule in such circumstances would be no small feat.

Saving effort is of course not the whole story in sustaining development. Saving must be channeled into productive investments that can underpin future welfare, rather than high-profile but ultimately nonremunerative projects. As Sarraf and Jiwanji (2001) document, Botswana's successful bid to avoid the resource curse was built upon a whole range of sound macroeconomic and sectoral policies, underpinned by a positive political economy.

Endnotes

1. See Auty (2001), ch. 1 for a good overview. One of the earliest studies was Sachs and Warner (1995).

2. See Hamilton and Hartwick (2005). This chapter builds upon Hamilton and others (forthcoming).

3. In support of the point that high natural resource rents are not necessarily invested in human capital, Gylfason (2001) shows that public expenditure on education relative to national income and gross secondary-school enrollment is inversely related to the share of natural capital in national wealth across countries. Natural capital appears to crowd out human capital.

4. A sensitivity test shows that these results hold by and large for most countries in the group. A change of the investment rule to 4 per cent of 1987 GDP affects qualitatively only those countries for which the change in produced capital was relatively small: Hungary, Finland, and Indonesia.

Annex

Table A4.1 Change in Produced Assets under Varying Rules for Genuine Investment (I^G)

	Produced capital in 2000, $bn (1995 dollars)	$I^G = 0$ % difference	I^G = 5% of 1987 GDP % difference	I^G >= 5% of 1987 GDP % difference	Rent per GDP average % (1970–2000)
Nigeria	53.5	358.9	413.6	413.6	32.6
Venezuela, R. B. de	175.9	272.1	326.1	326.1	27.7
Congo, Rep. of	13.9	57.0	78.0	116.9	25.2
Mauritania	3.0	112.3	153.7	154.0	25.0
Gabon	19.7	80.3	105.5	130.4	24.1
Trinidad and Tobago	13.7	182.1	238.3	239.1	23.6
Algeria	195.4	50.6	80.9	83.9	23.3
Bolivia	13.7	116.1	169.8	177.5	12.8
Indonesia	540.6	–26.5	3.8	32.1	12.5
Ecuador	37.7	95.3	158.0	158.3	11.6
Zambia	7.5	312.3	383.4	388.0	11.5
Guyana	2.1	149.3	185.6	191.2	11.4
China	2,899.4	–62.1	–45.0	5.1	10.8
Egypt, Arab Rep. of	159.7	–12.9	28.1	36.2	9.5
Chile	151.4	–3.0	31.6	54.0	9.5
Malaysia	305.2	–52.7	–31.4	6.6	8.3
Mexico	975.5	–1.5	35.3	42.2	8.2
Peru	132.3	37.2	98.1	103.9	7.5
Cameroon	24.1	–9.3	54.8	67.6	6.5
South Africa	349.5	50.7	109.3	115.8	6.5
Jamaica	13.4	39.9	87.8	99.6	5.7
Colombia	198.0	–19.7	30.4	39.3	5.3
Norway	456.6	–14.3	24.6	33.0	4.3
India	965.4	–52.9	–18.3	8.6	3.4
Zimbabwe	14.9	9.1	64.8	89.1	3.3
United States	16,926.7	–39.8	12.9	26.1	2.7
Argentina	569.6	–6.9	49.4	53.9	2.6
Togo	3.6	–26.8	22.7	55.1	2.6

	Produced capital in 2000, $bn (1995 dollars)	$I^G = 0$ % difference	I^G = 5% of 1987 GDP % difference	I^G >= 5% of 1987 GDP % difference	Rent per GDP average % (1970–2000)
Pakistan	125.6	–50.7	–1.7	11.1	2.2
Hungary	149.1	–43.5	8.7	22.3	2.2
Morocco	93.8	–59.1	–16.3	7.8	2.0
Brazil	1,750.5	–59.0	–6.6	9.1	1.9
United Kingdom	2,400.1	–32.7	27.3	32.8	1.6
Dominican Republic	33.8	–73.0	–27.9	1.2	1.6
Philippines	195.0	–58.4	–14.5	10.6	1.5
Honduras	12.3	–66.9	–29.7	8.9	1.5
Ghana	16.1	30.6	73.2	76.7	1.0
Fiji	3.6	–36.5	26.9	59.3	0.9
Benin	4.6	–72.7	–21.7	10.6	0.8
Senegal	10.0	–44.0	14.2	27.5	0.7
Thailand	520.6	–86.3	–63.6	3.0	0.7
Haiti	2.8	–62.7	109.2	109.5	0.6
Korea, Rep. of	1,607.6	–93.5	–68.6	0.9	0.6
Israel	215.8	–72.8	–31.3	4.2	0.5
Côte d'Ivoire	16.1	–21.2	71.1	108.7	0.5
Bangladesh	89.7	–59.0	–12.9	15.5	0.5
Rwanda	3.9	–83.2	–6.9	24.6	0.4
Sweden	508.0	–31.1	35.6	36.1	0.4
Nicaragua	6.9	–34.9	8.1	44.8	0.3
Spain	1,623.6	–58.9	–15.1	6.1	0.3
Denmark	437.2	–33.0	21.9	28.7	0.2
France	3,724.7	–55.0	–1.9	6.9	0.1
Italy	2,711.2	–44.8	7.5	10.2	0.1
Finland	347.6	–40.9	11.6	23.3	0.1
Belgium	681.9	–48.0	2.3	10.4	0.1
Niger	3.0	9.7	95.2	136.1	0.1
Burundi	1.6	–87.3	10.1	30.2	0.1
Portugal	308.8	–71.0	–30.8	5.7	0.0
Costa Rica	24.1	–80.0	–30.6	3.6	0.0

Continued

Table A4.1 (Continued)

	Produced capital in 2000, $bn (1995 dollars)	$I^G = 0$ % difference	I^G = 5% of 1987 GDP % difference	I^G >= 5% of 1987 GDP % difference	Rent per GDP average % (1970–2000)
El Salvador	17.1	–59.7	–2.5	24.6	0.0
Hong Kong, China	445.9	–88.6	–56.4	0.9	0.0
Kenya	20.1	–51.9	2.0	20.8	0.0
Madagascar	4.9	–26.9	62.4	65.5	0.0
Sri Lanka	41.2	–88.1	–55.4	1.0	0.0
Malawi	4.6	–26.8	9.4	68.2	0.0
Uruguay	29.9	–55.5	22.1	37.2	0.0
Luxembourg	43.3	–63.2	–22.0	15.7	0.0
Paraguay	23.7	–88.6	–46.6	3.0	0.0
Lesotho	5.7	–95.7	–79.9	0.1	0.0
Singapore	314.8	–92.7	–73.2	0.0	0.0

Source: Authors.

Note: Negative entries indicate that hypothetical produced assets would be lower than observed assets under the specified rule.

Chapter 5

The Importance of Population Dynamics: Changes in Wealth per Capita

Adjusted net, or genuine, saving was introduced in chapter 3. As a more-inclusive measure of net saving effort, one that includes depletion and degradation of the environment, depreciation of produced assets, and investments in human capital, genuine saving provides a useful indicator of sustainable development. The underlying theory (Hamilton and Clemens 1999) shows that negative rates of genuine saving imply future declines in utility along the optimal growth path for the economy. In the real world these theoretical results imply the common-sense notion that sustained negative rates of genuine saving must lead, eventually, to declining welfare. See box 1.1 for an overview of the theoretical work linking net saving to changes in welfare.

If population is not static, then it is clearly per capita welfare that policy should aim to sustain. Genuine saving measures the real change in value of total assets rather than the change in assets per capita. Genuine saving answers an important question: Did total wealth rise or fall over the accounting period? However, it does not speak directly to the question of the sustainability of economies when there is a growing population. If genuine saving is negative, then it is clear in both total and per capita terms that wealth is declining. For a range of countries, however, it is possible that genuine saving in total could be positive while wealth per capita is declining.

A simple formula, which assumes that the population grows exogenously, makes the accounting clear. If total wealth is denoted W, population P, and population growth rate g, then the change in wealth per capita can be shown to equal:

$$\Delta\left(\frac{W}{P}\right) = \frac{\Delta W}{P} - g \cdot \frac{W}{P} = \frac{W}{P}\left(\frac{\Delta W}{W} - g\right) \qquad (5.1)$$

If we interpret ΔW as genuine saving, then the first equality says that the change in wealth per capita equals genuine saving per capita minus a Malthusian term, the population growth rate times total wealth per capita. A growing population implies that existing wealth must be shared with each new cohort entering the population. More intuitively, the second equality in equation 5.1 says that total wealth per capita will rise or fall depending on whether the growth rate of total wealth ($\Delta W/W$) is higher or lower than the population growth rate.

This chapter applies the formula for changes in wealth per capita provided in equation 5.1 to the wealth database for the year 2000. The interplay of saving effort and population growth turns out to be quite significant.

Accounting for Changes in Wealth per Capita: A Ghanaian Example

Measuring saving and wealth in per capita terms requires some changes to the accounting framework presented in chapters 2 and 3. The first point is that we wish to measure only total *tangible* wealth, excluding intangible capital, when calculating the change in wealth per capita. Roughly speaking, the intuition behind this is that much intangible capital is *embodied* in the population.

An adjustment should be made to the calculation of adjusted net saving. The underlying accounting framework suggests that a growing population, through a Malthusian effect, as described above, should actually boost saving per person when the stock of carbon dioxide historically emitted by a given country is taken into account. This potentially offsets the effect of current emissions per person. Since no data on stocks of carbon dioxide emitted by country are available, we simplify the accounting by dropping value of emissions per person.

Table 5.1 Ghana: Calculating the Change in Wealth
— $ per capita —

Tangible wealth		Adjusted net saving	
Subsoil assets	65	Gross national saving	40
Timber resources	290	Education expenditure	7
NTFR	76	Consumption fixed capital	19
Protected areas	7	Energy depletion	0
Cropland	855	Mineral depletion	4
Pastureland	43	Net forest depletion	8
Produced capital	686		
Total tangible wealth	2022	Adjusted net saving	16
Population growth	1.7%	Δ Wealth per capita	–18

Source: Authors.
Note: Data for 2000. NTFR: nontimber forest resources.

Table 5.1 displays the detailed accounting of the change in wealth per capita in Ghana, a country with a 1.7 percent population growth rate per year. The left-hand column shows the assets that compose tangible wealth, summed to yield total tangible wealth per capita. The right-hand column breaks out the accounting of adjusted net saving. Gross national saving is added to education expenditures to yield total saving effort; consumption of fixed capital and natural resource depletion are then subtracted from this total to yield the net saving per Ghanaian, $16. The population growth rate is then multiplied by tangible wealth (the Malthusian term) and the result subtracted from adjusted net saving to yield the bottom-line change in wealth, –$18 per Ghanaian. The rate of change of total real wealth ($16/$2,022 = 0.8 percent) is less than the population growth rate.

Changes in Wealth per Capita in Selected African Countries

Table 5.2 summarizes the results of this accounting for the African countries in the wealth database. The gross national income (GNI) per capita and population growth rates are provided for reference in the table. Adjusted net saving excludes carbon dioxide emissions, as described above.

Table 5.2 Africa: Change in Wealth per Capita 2000

— $ per capita —

	GNI per capita	Population growth rate (%)	Adjusted net saving per capita	Change in wealth per capita	Saving gap (% GNI)
Benin	360	2.6	14	−42	11.5
Botswana	2,925	1.7	1,021	814	
Burkina Faso	230	2.5	15	−36	15.8
Burundi	97	1.9	−10	−37	37.7
Cameroon	548	2.2	−8	−152	27.7
Cape Verde	1,195	2.7	43	−81	6.8
Chad	174	3.1	−8	−74	42.6
Comoros	367	2.5	−17	−73	19.9
Congo, Rep. of	660	3.2	−227	−727	110.2
Côte d'Ivoire	625	2.3	−5	−100	16.0
Ethiopia	101	2.4	−4	−27	27.1
Gabon	3,370	2.3	−1,183	−2,241	66.5
Gambia, The	305	3.4	−5	−45	14.6
Ghana	255	1.7	16	−18	7.2
Kenya	343	2.3	40	−11	3.2
Madagascar	245	3.1	9	−56	22.7
Malawi	162	2.1	−2	−29	18.2
Mali	221	2.4	20	−47	21.2
Mauritania	382	2.9	−30	−147	38.4
Mauritius	3,697	1.1	645	514	
Mozambique	195	2.2	15	−20	10.0
Namibia	1,820	3.2	392	140	
Niger	166	3.3	−10	−83	50.3
Nigeria	297	2.4	−97	−210	70.6
Rwanda	233	2.9	14	−60	26.0
Senegal	449	2.6	31	−27	6.1
Seychelles	7,089	0.9	1,162	904	
South Africa	2,837	2.5	246	−2	0.1
Swaziland	1,375	2.5	129	8	
Togo	285	4.0	−20	−88	30.8
Zambia	312	2.0	−13	−63	20.4
Zimbabwe	550	2.0	53	−4	0.7

Source: Authors.

Note: All dollars at market exchange rates.

The table introduces a new performance indicator, the *saving gap* as a share of GNI. This is a measure of how much extra saving effort would be required in order for a country to break even with zero change in wealth per capita. It is calculated by identifying negative changes in wealth per capita, a measure of how far countries are from the break-even point, then dividing this by GNI per capita. South Africa is effectively at the point where wealth creation just offsets population growth.

This table shows that the generally high rates of population growth in African countries translate into very few countries with growing wealth per capita—Botswana,[1] Mauritius, Namibia, Seychelles, and Swaziland. These positive examples show that a Malthusian outcome is not inevitable. Sound resource policies combined with sound macroeconomic policies can lead to wealth creation.

A long list of African countries exhibits positive net saving per capita, but negative changes in total wealth per capita. These include Benin, Burkina Faso, Cape Verde, Ghana, Kenya, Madagascar, Mali, Mozambique, Rwanda, Senegal, and Zimbabwe. Population growth is outstripping wealth creation in these countries.

The oil states—the Republic of Congo, Gabon, and Nigeria—stand out in table 5.2 for enormous saving gaps (more than 100 percent of GNI in the case of the Republic of Congo). These countries are both running down total assets (as measured by negative adjusted net saving) and experiencing the immiserating effects of high population growth rates.

Changes in Wealth per Capita Across Countries

Figures 5.1 and 5.2 summarize changes in wealth per capita across all 118 countries in the database. The first figure scatters change in wealth per capita as a share of GNI against GNI per capita. The aim is to see how saving performance is linked to levels of income. The second figure looks at the correlation of net saving per capita with population growth rates.

As figure 5.1 shows, the broad picture is that the rich are getting richer while the poor are getting poorer. There is an upward trend to the scatter,

Figure 5.1 Change in Wealth per GNI vs. GNI per Capita, 2000

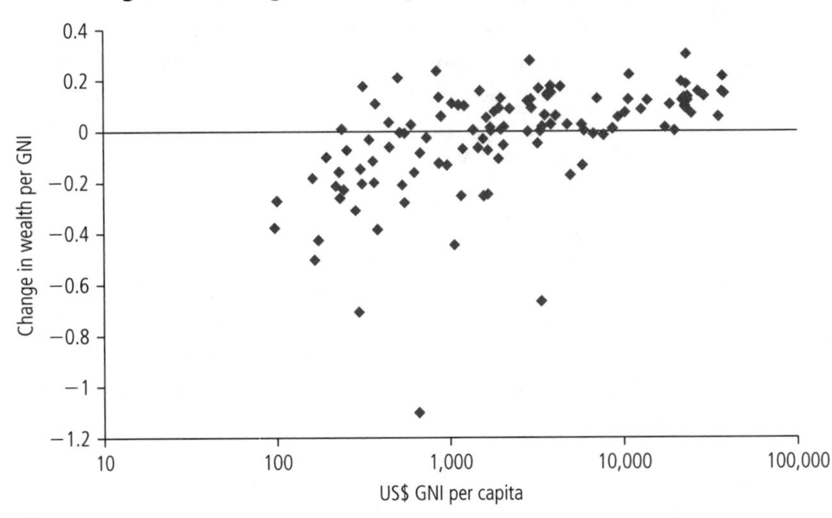

Source: Authors. Data on GNI per capita are from World Bank 2005.

and the majority of countries with GNI of less than $1,000 per person have declines in wealth per capita. Low levels of saving in poor countries are well-known phenomena, but factoring in population growth accentuates this trend markedly.

The downward trend in figure 5.2 shows that high population growth rates are associated with lower net accumulation of wealth per person. Empirically, the majority of countries with population growth rates above 1.5 percent a year are on a path of declining wealth per capita. The figure shows a cluster of countries with population growth rates between 2 percent and 3 percent and positive accumulation of wealth per capita. Countries such as Namibia, the Philippines, and Jordan show that, as noted above, Malthusian outcomes are not inevitable.

The table in appendix 4 reports results on changes in wealth per capita and saving gaps across all countries in the database, using the same structure as table 5.2.

The oil producers joining the list of countries with high saving gaps (greater than 10 percent of GNI) include Syria, Iran, Ecuador, Algeria, República Bolivariana de Venezuela, and Trinidad and Tobago. Both in total and on a per capita basis these countries are running down their assets. Studies of historical data have shown that

Figure 5.2 Change in Wealth per GNI vs. Population Growth Rate, 2000

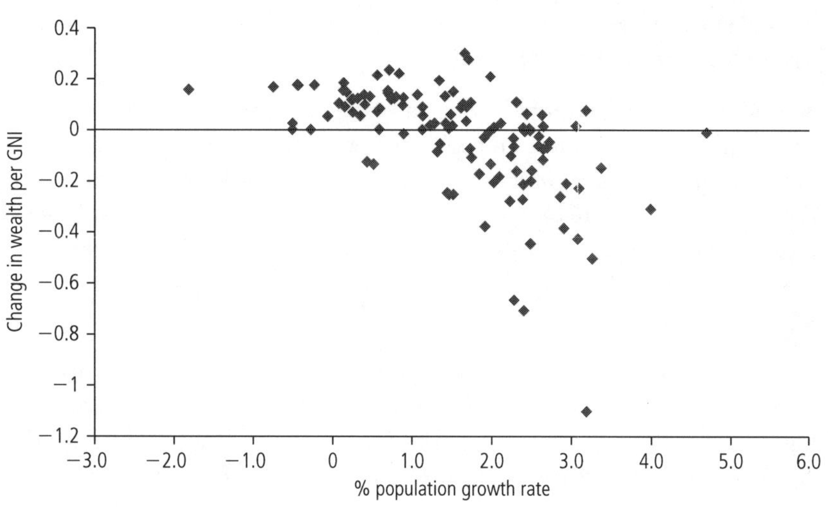

Source: Authors. Data on population growth are from World Bank 2005.

countries combining high dependence on resource extraction and negative net saving rates have lagged the growth performance of other countries (Atkinson and Hamilton 2003).

Finally, many of the countries of Eastern Europe and Central Asia are experiencing population declines, which raises saving per capita according to the formula underlying the saving calculation. These countries include Bulgaria, Estonia, Georgia, Hungary, Latvia, Moldova, Romania, and the Russian Federation. While, in principle, shrinking populations increase assets per capita, there is no guarantee that this will increase welfare per capita if these assets are not used efficiently.

Conclusions

Before drawing the main conclusions from this analysis, it is important to note some alternative models of adjusted net saving. First, one of the largest potential factors offsetting dissaving is technological change. If technological change can be considered to be exogenous, then the effect of growth in total factor productivity has to be built into the saving analysis. While for high-income countries the adjustment to saving could be very large,[2] total factor productivity growth in low-income countries has been extremely low or negative.

Second, if population growth were endogenous, then this could potentially have an impact on countries' prospects for future welfare. For example, if fertility were negatively related to wealth per person, then countries that are calculated to have negative changes in wealth per capita could potentially face higher birthrates and a downward spiral of immiseration. This would tend to emphasize the importance of the figures presented here.

The Ghanaian example shows that it is indeed possible to have positive genuine saving in total, but declining wealth per person. Countries with high population growth rates are effectively on a treadmill, and need to create new wealth just to maintain existing levels of wealth per capita.

Table 5.2 suggests very large saving gaps in Sub-Saharan Africa when population growth is taken into account. Excluding the oil states, saving gaps in many countries are on the order of 10–50 percent of GNI. Against this must be set the realization that reigning in government consumption by even a few percentage points of GNI is extremely painful and often politically perilous. Macroeconomic policies alone seem unlikely to close the gap.

The table in appendix 4 shows that large saving gaps are not strictly a Sub-Saharan African phenomenon. Selected countries in the Middle East and North Africa, Latin America and the Caribbean, East Asia, and South Asia also have significant saving gaps. Although wealth data are lacking, given their sharply negative genuine saving rates (reported in chapter 3) and moderate population growth rates, it is highly likely that the oil states in Central Asia (Azerbaijan, Kazakhstan, and Uzbekistan) also face large saving gaps.

Against this rather bleak picture there are the examples of countries that, even in the face of high population growth rates, have managed to achieve positive rates of wealth accumulation per capita. Policy clearly matters, both in the resource and macroeconomic domains. The next chapter examines, using historical data, whether the model of saving presented here is overstringent in its assumptions about the effects of population growth.

Endnotes

1. Botswana has relatively low population growth and a sizable increase in wealth per capita, but the lack of data on diamonds in the wealth database means that this is a highly distorted picture.

2. Weitzman and Löfgren (1997) calculate a boost to United States GDP on the order of 40 percent from exogenous technological changes. Total factor productivity measures the contribution to economic growth that cannot be strictly attributed to accumulation of produced capital or labor.

Chapter 6

Testing Genuine Saving

Intuition suggests that saving today should have an effect on future economic performance, and indeed, the large body of work on across-country analysis of economic growth supports this (Sala-i-Martin 1997; Hamilton 2005; Ferreira and others 2003; Ferreira and Vincent 2005). The literature on genuine saving makes a prediction that is eminently testable: current saving should equal the change over the accounting period in the present value of future well-being along the optimal growth path of the economy. The proposition that net saving is equal to changes in well-being has been proved in the literature. See box 1.1 for more details.

The empirical test of this prediction exploits the 30-plus-year time series on genuine saving described in chapter 3 and published every year in the *World Development Indicators* (WDI) (World Bank 2005). With these historical data it is possible to ask whether measured genuine saving in 1980 actually equaled the present value of changes in consumption as measured in the consumption time series. While the data may not fit the theory perfectly for any individual country, the analysis is carried out across countries to see whether statistically there is a good fit of the data to the theory.

One problem with designing an empirical test concerns the restrictiveness of the underlying model of the economy. Many of the models in the literature on saving and sustainability assume optimality, in the sense of the economy actually maximizing the present value of social well-being at each point in time, as well as fixed interest rates and constant returns to scale. Each of these assumptions is likely to be violated in real-world economies, which limits the feasibility of testing the models with historical data.

These difficulties notwithstanding, testing alternative measures of saving is important if policy makers are to be convinced to use a measure such as genuine saving as a performance measure for the economy.

Specifying the Empirical Test

Recent theoretical work provides a model of the linkage between saving and future well-being that shares few of the theoretical restrictions of earlier work (Hamilton and Hartwick 2005; Hamilton and Withagen 2004). Two basic assumptions are required:

- Economies are competitive, in the sense that producers are free to maximize profits, while households are free to maximize well-being.
- Externalities are internalized. For example, pollution taxes are employed to ensure that prices reflect the damages that producers inflict on households when a pollutant is emitted.

The first assumption is valid for many economies. The second assumption is valid for relatively few economies, but the empirical literature on pollution damages suggests that the size of the impact is likely to be small in most economies.

Under these assumptions it is possible to define the following basic relationship between the measure of change in total real wealth per capita G and changes in consumption C per capita:

$$G_0 = \sum_{t=1}^{T} \frac{1}{(1+r)^t} \cdot \left(\frac{C_t}{N_t} - \frac{C_{t-1}}{N_{t-1}} \right) \tag{6.1}$$

Here N is total population, r is the discount rate, and T is an assumed time period for the analysis. This expression just says that current change in total wealth per capita should equal the present value of changes in consumption per capita.

Assuming this relationship holds, then it is possible to test it econometrically as:

$$PVC_i = \alpha + \beta \cdot G_i + \varepsilon_i \tag{6.2}$$

where G_i is one of several alternative measures of saving for country i, while PVC_i is the present value of changes in future consumption as suggested by the expression above. If the data fit the theory, then we would expect $\alpha = 0$ and $\beta = 1$.

The World Bank's time series of saving data permit tests of alternative measures of saving. Four different measures are tested, as follows:

- *Gross* saving is just gross national income (GNI) minus total consumption in the private and public sectors—it is the amount of output that is not consumed in any given year. Gross saving is the figure typically reported and used by ministries of finance.
- *Net* saving deducts the depreciation of produced capital from gross saving.
- *Adjusted net* or *genuine* saving deducts the depletion of natural resources and pollution damages from net saving.
- *Malthusian* saving[1] measures the change in total real wealth per capita as defined in chapter 5—it is equal to genuine saving per capita, minus the population growth rate times the value of tangible wealth per capita.

Data and Methodology of Estimation

The time series data for the analysis—GNI, gross saving, consumption of fixed capital,[2] and depletion of natural resources (energy, minerals, and net forest depletion)—are taken directly from the WDI (World Bank 2005). Total tangible wealth, employed in the Malthusian saving calculation, is derived using a perpetual inventory model (PIM) for produced capital stock estimates (the same model used in arriving at the total wealth estimates for 2000 presented in chapter 2 and elsewhere); present values of mineral and energy rents; and present values of forestry, fishing, and agricultural rents, all measured in constant 1995 dollars (Ferreira and others 2003).

Public expenditures on education are excluded from the genuine and Malthusian saving measures. These were shown to perform exceedingly badly in earlier econometric tests of saving by Ferreira and Vincent (2005). There are a number of plausible reasons for the poor performance:

- These are gross, rather than net, investment estimates.
- Private education expenditures are excluded.
- Expenditures may be a very poor proxy for human capital formation, particularly in developing countries (Pritchett 1996).

Damages from carbon dioxide emissions are also excluded from the saving measures. This is partly because the bulk of the damages occur in the longer term, but also because, in the absence of a binding agreement to pay compensation, damages to other countries (the major effect of emitting carbon dioxide) should have no effect on future consumption in the emitting country.

One of the key choices to be made in estimating the expression for saving econometrically is the choice of period over which to calculate changes in consumption. The underlying theory suggests that there is, in principle, an infinite time horizon. As a practical matter, however, the data on genuine saving are limited to the period 1970–2000, with data for the early 1970s being particularly sparse.

A reasonable choice of time horizon would be the mean lifetime of produced capital stocks, roughly 20 years (machinery and equipment lifetimes are typically shorter, 10 years or so, but buildings and infrastructure have lifetimes of several decades). Choosing 20 years would be saying, in effect, that the effects of saving will be felt over the lifetime of the produced capital in which they are presumed to be invested. This is the assumption used below, and testing the estimation for a 10-year time horizon produced less robust estimates overall (in terms of explained variation, probability of rejecting a linear relationship between dependent and independent variables, and significance of the coefficients on saving).

The other decision required for estimation concerns the discount rate. The underlying theory (Ferreira and others 2003) suggests that the rate should be the marginal product of capital, less depreciation rates for produced capital, less population growth rates, which argues for a low value. We use a uniform rate of 5 percent, and tests of alternatives suggest that the estimates are fairly insensitive to small changes in the discount rate.

Allowing for the sparse early-1970s saving data,[3] therefore, the regression equation was estimated using Ordinary Least Squares (OLS) for consecutive 20-year periods from 1976 to 1980. These results, as well as more informal methods, are reported below.

Empirical Results

To provide a feel for the data, we first scatter the present value of changes in consumption against the four different saving measures for 1980 in figures 6.1–6.4. The broad picture which emerges is that there is no monotonic improvement in the fit with theory as more stringent measures of saving are applied. The coefficient on saving actually drops from gross saving to net saving, and the explained variation drops considerably. For genuine saving the coefficient on saving is higher and very near one. Finally, for Malthusian saving the coefficient on saving drops to the lowest level of the four measures, while explained variation reaches its highest value.

Figure 6.5 presents the same scatter for high-income countries only. As seen in Ferreira and Vincent (2005) and Ferreira and others (2003), the model fit is particularly poor for these countries. Further tests show the coefficient on saving to be insignificant, while the explained variation is very low.

Figure 6.1 Present Value of Change in Consumption vs. Gross Saving, 1980

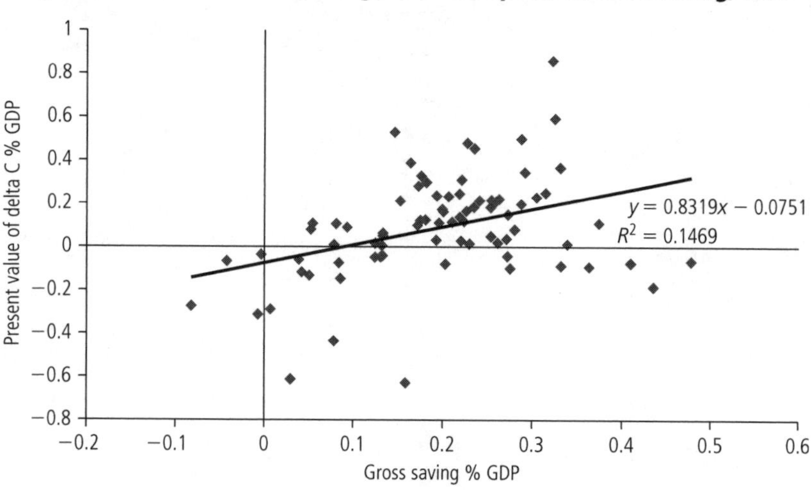

Source: Authors.

Figure 6.2 Present Value of Change in Consumption vs. Net Saving, 1980

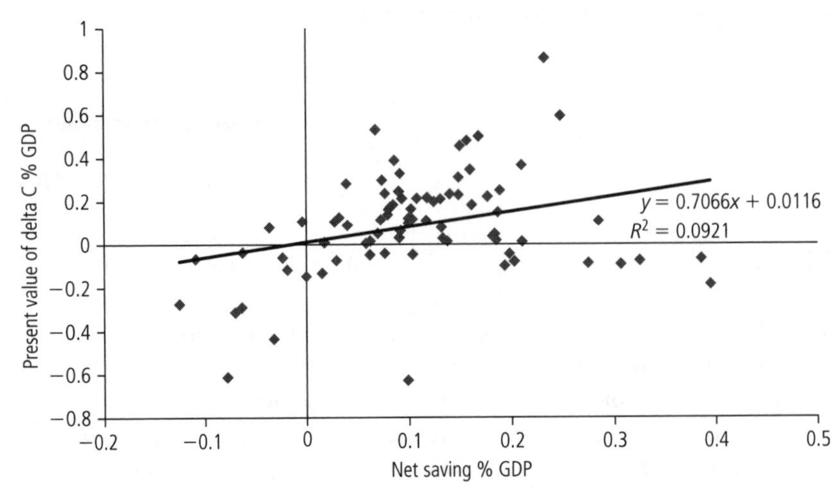

Source: Authors.

Figure 6.3 Present Value of Change in Consumption vs. Genuine Saving, 1980

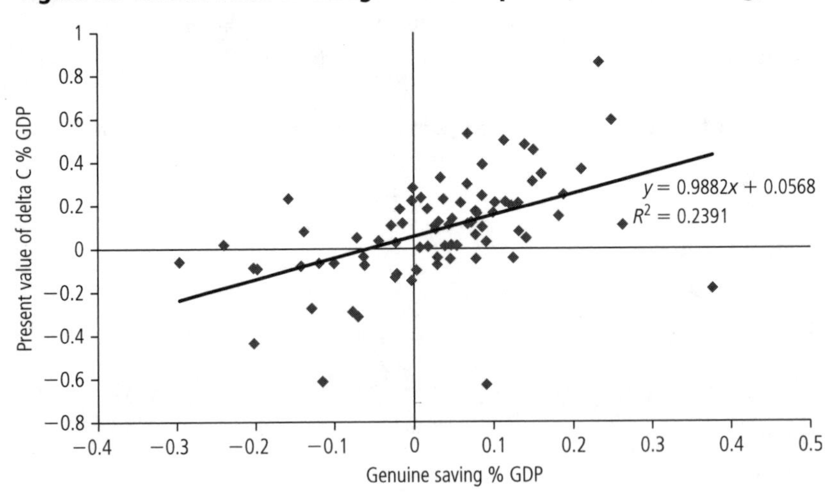

Source: Authors.

Figure 6.4 Present Value of Change in Consumption vs. Malthusian Saving, 1980

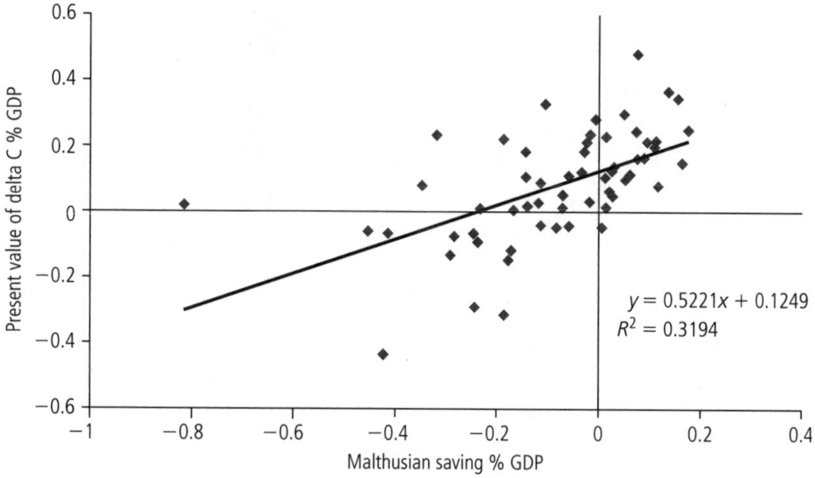

Present value of delta C % GDP
0.6
0.4
0.2
0
−0.2
−0.4
−0.6
−1
−0.8
−0.6
−0.4
−0.2
0
0.2
0.4
Malthusian saving % GDP
y = 0.5221x + 0.1249
R2 = 0.3194

Source: Authors.

Figure 6.5 Present Value of Change in Consumption vs. Genuine Saving, High-Income Countries, 1980

Present value of delta C % GDP
0.4
0.35
0.3
0.25
0.2
0.15
0.1
0.05
0
−0.05
0
0.05
0.1
0.15
0.2
Genuine saving % GDP

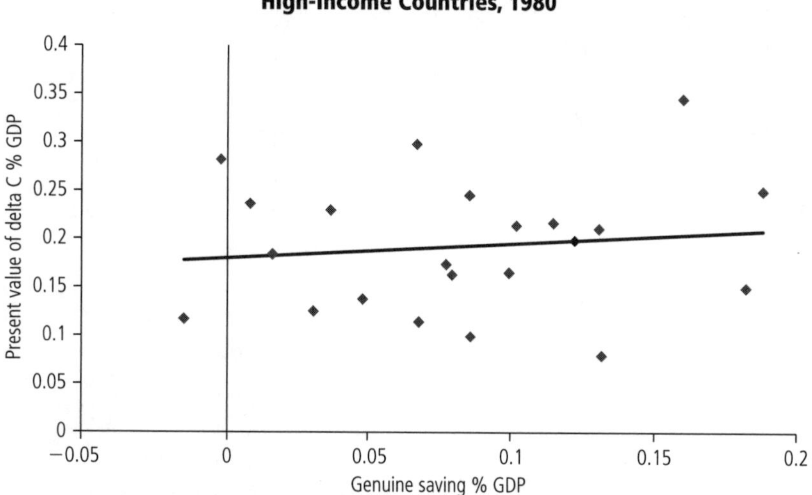

Source: Authors.

Table 6.1 Regression Results for PVC = alpha + beta × Saving

	1976		1977		1978		1979		1980	
	beta	alpha	beta	alpha	beta	alpha	beta	alpha	beta	alpha
Gross saving										
Coeff.	1.0152	−0.0737	0.7596	−0.0338	1.0484	−0.1212	1.2325	−0.1743	0.8319	−0.0751
tstat	3.0335	−0.9511	2.4358	−0.4628	3.7257	−1.8992	4.7372	−2.8601	3.6416	−1.4656
R^2	0.1479		0.0803		0.1598		0.2351		0.1469	
Df	53		68		73		73		77	
Pr > F	0.0037		0.0175		0.0004		0.0000		0.0005	
beta = 1	0.0445		−0.7595		0.1697		0.8814		−0.7264	
Net saving										
Coeff.	0.6634	0.0606	0.2161	0.1047	0.6485	0.0209	0.9835	−0.0293	0.7066	0.0116
tstat	1.7723	1.0787	0.6471	2.0414	1.9740	0.4433	3.2791	−0.6574	2.7943	0.3102
R^2	0.0560		0.0061		0.0507		0.1284		0.0921	
Df	53		68		73		73		77	
Pr > F	0.0821		0.5198		0.0522		0.0016		0.0066	
beta = 1	−0.8823		−2.3125		−1.0555		−0.0542		−1.1451	
Genuine saving										
Coeff.	1.2803	0.0483	0.8532	0.0677	1.2553	0.0131	0.7815	0.0580	0.9882	0.0568
tstat	4.5524	1.4442	3.4246	2.1915	4.9943	0.4654	4.2716	2.3469	4.9187	2.3175
R^2	0.2811		0.1471		0.2547		0.2000		0.2391	
Df	53		68		73		73		77	
Pr > F	0.0000		0.0010		0.0000		0.0001		0.0000	
beta = 1	0.9780		−0.5808		1.0019		−1.1781		−0.0578	
Malthusian saving										
Coeff.	0.7757	0.1337	0.5741	0.1200	0.4663	0.1061	0.3599	0.1117	0.5221	0.1249
tstat	3.8801	5.1418	3.2489	5.0664	4.0371	5.0553	3.7425	5.2683	5.1265	6.1294
R^2	0.2785		0.1772		0.2352		0.2030		0.3194	
Df	39		49		53		55		56	
Pr > F	0.0004		0.0021		0.0002		0.0004		0.0000	
beta = 1	−1.0937		−2.3613		−4.5343		−6.5358		−4.6100	

Source: Authors.

Table 6.1 presents the results of the individual OLS estimates of the model for each of the five years and four measures of saving. This table reports the coefficient values with t-statistics, R-squared, degrees of freedom, the probability of rejecting a linear relationship (from the F statistic), and a simple two-sided t-test of whether the coefficient on saving is equal to 1 (values greater than 2.00 imply the coefficient is significantly different from 1 at the 5 percent confidence level). While there is some heterogeneity in the results, the following broad conclusions hold:

- The results for 1977 are the weakest of the five years, with low R-squared, higher probabilities of rejecting a linear relationship than other years, and two saving coefficient estimates that are significantly different from one (although the coefficient for net saving is not itself significant). This suggests some systematic shock being picked up by the data for this year.
- Results for net saving are generally the weakest of the four saving measures tested, with insignificant coefficients on saving at the 5 percent level in 1976 and 1977, and generally low R-squared and higher probability of rejecting a linear relationship than other measures.
- Malthusian saving exhibits the worst fit with theory, with the coefficients on saving being the lowest of the four saving measures, and significantly different from one in four out of the five years tested.
- The results for gross and genuine saving have similarities, with the coefficients on saving being significant and not significantly different from one in all years. Genuine saving explains much more of the total variation in four out of five years, and exhibits lower probability of rejecting a linear relationship in the same four years, suggesting a more robust fit with theory.

Quantitative analysis suggests a moderate advantage to using genuine saving as a predictor of future welfare, in the sense of a one percentage-point change in saving translating into a 1 percent change in the present value of changes in future consumption. Figures 6.1 and 6.3 suggest a more qualitative test. In Figure 6.1 it can readily be seen that gross saving provides many *false positives* in the form of positive base-year saving translating into negative welfare outcomes—these are the scatter points lying in the lower-right quadrant. Similarly, the upper-left quadrant points in figure 6.3 represent *false negatives*—countries where negative base-year genuine saving was associated with increases in welfare.

Table 6.2 False Signals regarding Future Changes in Consumption (ratios)

	1976	1977	1978	1979	1980	Wt. avg.
Gross saving						
False positive	0.241	0.246	0.320	0.360	0.267	0.294
False negative	1.000	0.000	0.000	0.000	0.000	0.167
Net saving						
False positive	0.226	0.250	0.275	0.338	0.209	0.266
False negative	0.500	0.500	0.167	0.250	0.167	0.231
Genuine saving						
False positive	0.188	0.200	0.226	0.293	0.154	0.218
False negative	0.429	0.400	0.231	0.412	0.407	0.378
Malthusian saving						
False positive	0.043	0.080	0.037	0.077	0.043	0.056
False negative	0.611	0.615	0.464	0.452	0.600	0.543

Source: Authors.

Table 6.2 assembles the proportions of false positives and false negatives[4] for all saving measures, for all years, along with an average for each saving measure weighted by the number of countries with positive or negative saving observed. A few observations:

- Malthusian saving has the lowest proportion of false positives, but in fact, the vast majority of the countries with positive Malthusian saving are developed countries. The result is therefore unsurprising. This saving measure also has the highest proportion of false negatives, which is consistent with the results of the quantitative analysis.
- Gross and net saving have relatively low proportions of false negatives, but this represents very few countries (only one in the case of gross saving) across all years. There are simply very few countries with negative gross or net saving.
- Genuine saving has lower proportions of false positives than either gross or net saving, but this is balanced by a much higher proportion of false negatives.

Conclusions

Growth theory provides the basis for a stringent test of whether saving does, in fact, translate into future welfare. This chapter confronts the theory with real-world data—with positive results for measures of gross and genuine saving. Even without appealing to theoretical models, it may be asked when a dollar is saved how it could *not* show up in future production and consumption. Many answers to this question are possible:

- Saving may be measured very badly.
- Funds appropriated for public investments may not, in fact, be invested, owing to problems of governance.
- Investments, particularly by the public sector, may not be productive.

It is important to note the many caveats pertaining to this analysis. First, measurement error may be significant, particularly for consumption of fixed capital (where government estimates may be incorrect), depletion of natural resources (where World Bank resource rent estimates depend on rather sparse cost of extraction data, and where the methodology probably inflates the value of depletion for countries with large resource deposits), and total wealth estimates (especially produced capital in developing countries, where public investments may be particularly inefficient [Pritchett 2000]).

Missing variable bias may also be an issue. Although human capital is excluded from the analysis for the reasons outlined above, in principle, net investment in human capital should be an important contributor to future welfare. However, the negative effects of including education spending in the analysis of saving and future welfare in Ferreira and Vincent (2005) and Ferreira and others (2003) may simply be another manifestation of the small or negative growth impact of public education spending in developing countries analyzed by Pritchett (1996). In addition, for some countries, the exclusion of natural resources such as diamonds and fish may be a significant omission.

Exogenous shocks may present problems for testing the theory of saving and social welfare. The period under analysis in this chapter includes, in the early and least heavily discounted stages, the second oil shock in 1979 and a steep worldwide recession in 1981. However, Ferreira and others (2003) do not find any significant effects of exchange rate shocks in their analysis of the theory.

It should be noted that the theory being tested is particularly stringent, since it implies that measuring positive or negative saving *at a point in time* leads to future welfare being higher or lower than current welfare over some interval of time. In the real world, a positive exogenous shock (such as an improvement in the terms of trade) in the year immediately following the time when saving turned negative could easily swamp the effect of negative saving, and conversely for positive saving and negative shocks.

Turning to the results of the analysis, we find that the various saving measures are poor at signaling future changes in welfare in developed countries, similar to what Ferreira and Vincent (2005) and Ferreira and others (2003) find. This probably reflects factors other than capital accumulation being key for the growth performance of these economies: in particular, technological innovation, learning by doing, creation of institutional capital, and so on.

For all countries combined, we find that both net and Malthusian saving fit the theory poorly. The significantly low coefficients on Malthusian saving suggest that this measure overstates the effects of population growth on wealth accumulation per capita. Gross and genuine saving perform well, with estimated coefficients not being significantly different from the predicted values and with lower probabilities of rejecting a linear relationship between dependent and independent variables than for other measures. Genuine saving performs better than gross saving in terms of goodness of fit.

In terms of the more qualitative question of false positives and negatives, genuine saving provides, on average, a lower false-positive ratio than gross saving (22 percent of countries with positive genuine saving at a point in time actually experienced welfare declines, compared with 29 percent of countries with positive gross saving). Conversely, on average, negative genuine saving falsely signaled future welfare decreases in 38 percent of cases.

The bottom line is that genuine saving, excluding adjustments for population growth and education expenditure, is a good predictor of changes in future welfare as measured by consumption per capita. This result does not hold for high-income countries as a group, where factors other than simple asset accumulation are clearly driving future welfare. For developing countries the processes of accumulating produced assets and depleting natural resources clearly do influence their prospects for welfare.

Endnotes

1. While *Malthusian saving* is not a standard textbook saving measure, the name is useful and evocative for the purposes of this chapter.

2. Ferreira and others (2003) use estimated figures for consumption of fixed capital derived from the perpetual inventory model used to estimate total stocks of produced capital. Inspection of these figures reveals a fairly large number of anomalous estimates.

3. From 1970 to 1975 there are fewer than 40 countries with the necessary data, and these are primarily developed countries.

4. This is clearly a rather ad hoc test, but one that policy makers may care about.

PART 3

Wealth, Production, and Development

Chapter 7

Explaining the Intangible Capital Residual: The Role of Human Capital and Institutions

The Meaning of Intangible Capital

Chapter 2 showed that in most countries *intangible capital* is the largest share of total wealth. What does intangible capital measure in the wealth estimates? By construction, it captures all those assets that are not accounted for elsewhere. It includes human capital, the skills and know-how embodied in the labor force. It encompasses social capital, that is, the degree of trust among people in a society and their ability to work together for common purposes. It also includes those governance elements that boost the productivity of the economy. For example, if an economy has a very efficient judicial system, clear property rights, and an effective government, the result will be a higher total wealth and thus an increase in the intangible capital residual.

As a residual, intangible capital necessarily includes other assets which, for lack of data coverage, could not be accounted in the wealth estimates. As mentioned in chapter 2, one form of wealth is net foreign financial assets. When a country receives interest on the foreign bonds it owns, this boosts consumption and hence total wealth and the intangible capital residual. A similar argument applies to countries with net foreign obligations—to the extent that interest is being paid to foreigners, the residual will be lower. So while there are no comprehensive cross-country data on net foreign financial assets, this variable is measured implicitly in the intangible wealth residual for each country.

Finally, the intangible capital residual also includes any errors and omissions in the estimation of produced and natural capital. The main omissions include fisheries and subsoil water.

Figure 7.1 The Meaning of the Intangible Capital Residual

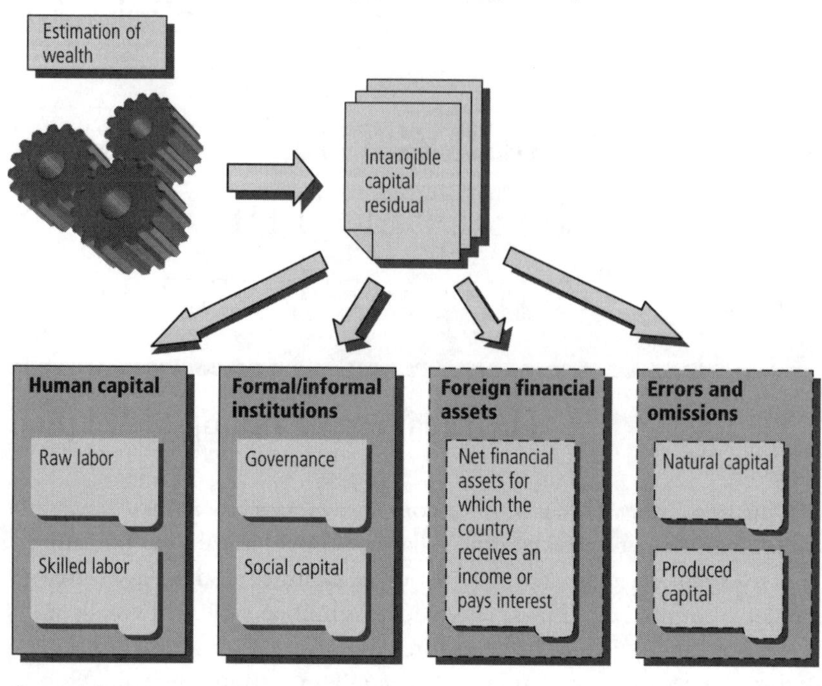

Source: Authors.

Keeping in mind the caveats above, the goal in this chapter is to disaggregate the intangible capital residual into its major components. The omission of foreign financial assets and some natural resources is not systematic, in that countries may differ widely in their endowments of such assets. For this reason we will concentrate on the more systematic contributors to the residual, such as human capital and institutional quality. The decomposition analysis in the following sections makes it possible to measure the residual as a set of specific assets; these assets in turn may be subject to specific policy measures.

Among the components of intangible capital, perhaps the one that has been most widely analyzed in the economics literature is human capital. For example, table 7.1 shows how growth in output per capita in the Organisation for Economic Co-operation and Development (OECD) countries compares to growth in inputs and in total factor productivity. Growth in labor quality explains an important part of the

Table 7.1 Growth in Output and Input per Capita in OECD Countries (percentage)

1960–95	USA	Canada	UK	France	Germany	Italy	Japan
Growth in output per capita	2.11	2.24	1.89	2.68	2.66	3.19	4.81
Growth in capital stock per capita	1.35	2.35	2.69	3.82	3.76	4.01	3.49
Growth in hours worked per capita	0.42	0.14	–0.50	–0.99	–0.67	–0.17	0.35
Growth in labor quality	0.60	0.55	0.44	0.85	0.43	0.31	0.99
Growth in productivity	0.76	0.57	0.80	1.31	1.33	1.54	2.68

Source: Jorgensen and Yip 2001.

high rates of growth in output, but productivity growth is still a major component.

Box 7.1 provides a brief and nonexhaustive overview of what is meant by human capital and its measurement.

Box 7.1 The Measurement of Human Capital

While there is currently no monetary measure of human capital, this area of research promises to be very rewarding. Behrman and Taubman (1982, 474) define human capital as "the stock of economically productive human capabilities." Human capital can be increased through education expenditure, on-the-job training, and investments in health and nutrition. The difficulties in measuring human capital are linked to the fact that human capital is accumulated in a variety of ways. Not all of these contributions to human capital formation are easily measured. Even in the cases in which it is possible to have a measure, years of schooling for example, the effect on values of human capital may vary from country to country.

Physical Measures of Human Capital

The most basic measure of human capital is the average years of education for the population or the labor force. Schultz (1961) and Becker (1964) introduced the explicit treatment of education as an investment in human capital. Schultz (1988) provides a comprehensive analysis of the relationship between investments in human capital and income. Growth accounting exercises show that high levels of education explain high levels of output. The figure below displays this point by plotting average years of education against gross national income (GNI) per capita.

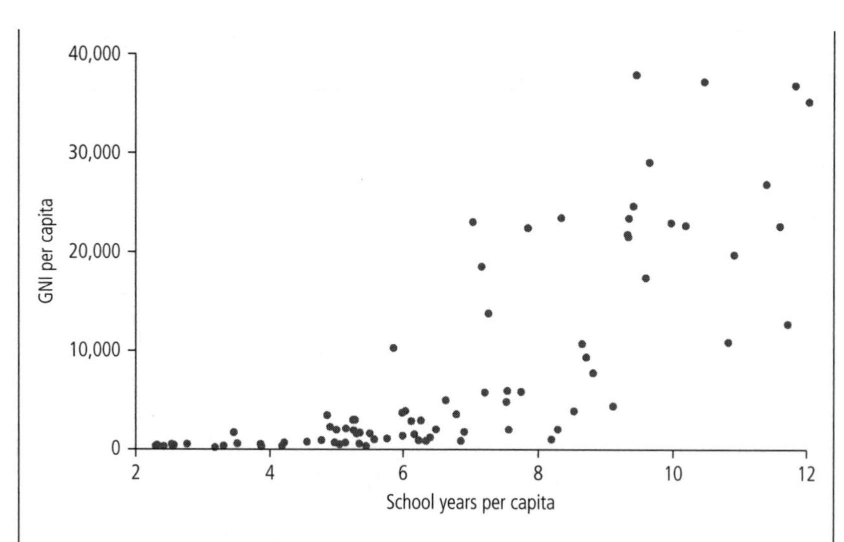

Source: Data on GNI per capita are from World Bank 2005. Data on school years are from Barro and Lee 2000.

Even taking into account years of schooling in growth accounting equations, a large unexplained difference in income across countries persists (Caselli 2003). For this reason, average school year measures are often complemented by attainment ratios, that is, the percentage of the relevant population that completes a given level of education (for example, primary, secondary, higher level). A comprehensive data set covering both school years and attainment is available from Barro and Lee (2000) and it has been used in the quantitative analysis here.

The use of schooling as a proxy for human capital implicitly assumes that one year of schooling in country A produces the same amount of human capital as one year of schooling in country B. If a more accurate measure of human capital is desired, the *quality* of education should be taken into account. This can be achieved by considering variables such as the quality of the teachers, the availability of teaching materials, the student-teacher ratio, test scores, and so on. All these measures are difficult to collect, and country-level data are not widely available.

Toward Monetary Measures of Human Capital

Human capital is the result of investments in improving the skills and knowledge of the labor force. A major step forward in the monetary valuation of human capital is therefore the estimation of the returns to such investments. Psacharopoulos and Patrinos (2004) provide comprehensive measures of the profitability of investment in education across countries. Among their findings is the fact that primary education produces the highest returns in low-income countries. The table below summarizes the results by income group. The entries in the table provide the return to one extra dollar spent on education. Returns decline with the level of schooling—that is, one dollar spent on primary school provides higher returns than one dollar spent on higher education—and with per capita income. The authors show that investments in education constitute a very profitable policy option.

Returns to Investment in Education by Level

	Social returns to education investments, %		
Country group	Primary	Secondary	Higher
Low-income countries	21.3	15.7	11.2
Middle-income countries	18.8	12.9	11.3
High-income countries	13.4	10.3	9.5
World	18.9	13.1	10.8

Source: Psacharopoulos and Patrinos 2004.

The usefulness of the rate of returns on education is very much under scrutiny. Using data for Sweden, Bjorklund and Kjellstrom (2002) find, for example, that results may be driven by the structure imposed by the estimation models. Further investigation is needed to refine such calculations.

Even if reliable data on rates of return were available, the estimation of human capital would require a baseline, that is, a starting level to which we can add successive investments in human capital to obtain the total value of human capital in any given moment in time. Wages for unskilled labor provide a conceptually sensible baseline, but comparable cross-country data are not available.

In the following section we will look at the broader intangible capital residual and attempt to disaggregate the effects of education and other variables, including governance. This will provide a first indication of the relative importance of the assets that constitute the residual.

A Regression Analysis of the Intangible Capital Residual

The intangible capital residual forces us to think of all contributors to wealth other than produced and natural capital. What are left are those assets that are more intangible and less prone to be measured.

Regression analysis can help us pinpoint the major determinants of the intangible capital residual.

Human capital must clearly be an important part of any model specification. A readily available proxy for human capital is schooling. Schooling level per person constitutes an imperfect measure of human capital, since it does not take into account the quality of education of those trained, nor other types of human capital investment such as on-the-job training. Measurement errors of this kind need not bias the coefficient, but would affect the significance. Average years of schooling per capita are used here for lack of better data.

A special form of human capital is represented by workers who have emigrated and send money to their families in the form of remittances. Even if they are not physically present in the country, workers abroad contribute to the country's income and hence they are a part of total national wealth. For this reason we also include remittances in our model.

Institutional quality is another important dimension that needs to be captured. Kaufmann, Kraay, and Mastruzzi (2005) provide data on six dimensions of governance:

- Voice and accountability
- Political stability and absence of violence
- Government effectiveness
- Regulatory quality
- Rule of law
- Control of corruption

The model below uses the rule of law indicator. This measures the extent to which agents have confidence in and abide by the rules of society. It encompasses the respect of citizens and the state for the institutions which govern their interactions. While there is no strong reason to prefer one governance dimension over another, an argument in favor of choosing the rule of law indicator is that it captures particularly well some of the features of a country's social capital. Paldam and Svendsen (forthcoming) associate social capital with trust, and report a *generalized trust* indicator for 20 countries. The correlation between generalized trust and rule of law is high, as shown in table 7.2.[1] The interpretation of the coefficients, in the analysis below, should then be subject to the caveat that there are several underlying elements explaining the association between rule of law and the intangible capital residual.

Table 7.2 Correlation Matrix of Social Capital and Governance Dimensions

	Trust	Voice	Stab	Goveff	Regqua	Rulelaw	Corr
Trust	1.000						
Voice	0.397	1.000					
Stab	0.309	0.675	1.000				
Goveff	0.482	0.506	0.868	1.000			
Regqua	0.240	0.450	0.807	0.878	1.000		
Rulelaw	0.514	0.560	0.908	0.945	0.868	1.000	
Corr	0.517	0.595	0.892	0.965	0.865	0.975	1.000

Sources: The trust indicator is taken from Paldam and Svendsen (forthcoming). The six governance dimensions are taken from Kaufmann, Kraay, and Mastruzzi (2005).
Notes: Voice: voice and accountability; Stab: political stability and absence of violence; Goveff: government effectiveness; Regqua: regulatory quality; Rulelaw: rule of law; Corr: control of corruption.

Our model represents the residual as a function of domestic human capital, as captured by the per capita years of schooling of the working population; human capital abroad, as captured by the amount of remittances by workers outside the country; and governance/social capital, expressed here as a rule of law index. We considered a simple Cobb-Douglas function:

$$R = AS^{\alpha_S} F^{\alpha_F} L^{\alpha_L} \tag{7.1}$$

where R is the intangible residual, A is a constant, S is years of schooling per worker, F is remittances from abroad and L is the rule of law index (measured on a scale of 1 to 100). The coefficients α_i express the elasticity of the residual with respect to the explanatory variables on the right-hand side of the equation above. So, for example, α_S measures the percentage increase in R if schooling is increased by 1 percent. There is also a set of income group dummy variables that take into account differences in the residual linked to income levels.

Elasticities

As table 7.3 shows, the specified model fits the data well. The independent variables explain 89 percent of the variations in the residual.

Table 7.3 Elasticities of Intangible Capital with Respect to Schooling, Remittances from Abroad, and Rule of Law

Variable	Coefficient	Standard error
School years	0.53	0.2162
Remittances from abroad	0.12	0.0472
Rule of law	0.83	0.3676
Low-income dummy	–2.54	0.4175
Lower-middle-income dummy	–1.90	0.2911
Upper-middle-income dummy	–1.55	0.2693
Constant	7.24	1.6005

Source: Authors.

Note: Dependent variable: log of intangible capital. Observations included: 79. R-squared: 0.89. Excluded dummy: high-income countries. All coefficients are significant at the 5 percent level.

All the coefficients estimated are significantly[2] different from zero at the 5 percent level and positive. The estimation suggests that a 1 percent increase in school years will increase the intangible capital residual by 0.53 percent. A 1 percent increase in the rule of law index is associated with a 0.83 percent increase in the residual. A coefficient lower than one in the model above means that there are decreasing marginal returns to the corresponding factor—for example, one more year of schooling yields higher returns in those countries with lower levels of schooling.

In addition, all the income dummy coefficients are negative. This means that countries in each income group have a lower level of intangible capital residual compared with high-income countries.

We also tested the hypothesis that the sum of the coefficients for schooling, remittances, and rule of law is equal to one. Statistically, this hypothesis cannot be rejected. In other words, if we imagine the three dependent variables as inputs in the production of intangible capital, then this production function exhibits constant returns to scale.

Marginal Returns

Using the elasticities obtained in the regression, it is possible to obtain marginal returns, that is, the unit change in the residual resulting from a unit change in the explanatory variable. In the case of Cobb-Douglas functions, marginal returns, or partial derivatives are easily obtained as:

$$\frac{\delta R}{\delta X} = \alpha_X \frac{R}{X} \tag{7.2}$$

Notice that while the elasticity α_X is constant, the marginal returns depend on the level of R and X. We evaluated marginal returns using the mean estimates for R and X in each income group. The information is summarized in table 7.4.

Table 7.4 Variation in Intangible Capital Resulting from a Unit Variation in the Explanatory Variables, by Income Group ($ per capita)

	Marginal returns to schooling	Marginal returns to rule of law	Marginal returns to foreign remittances
Low-income countries	838	111	29
Lower-middle-income countries	1,721	362	27
Upper-middle-income countries	2,398	481	110
High-income OECD countries	16,430	2,973	306

Source: Authors.

At the mean level of schooling, a one-year increase in schooling in low-income countries corresponds to a US$838 increase in the residual. In comparison, low-income countries spend nearly US$51 per student per year in primary school (World Bank 2005). This information provides useful insight for policy makers, especially when it comes to comparing costs and benefits of a given policy. With respect to the rule of law variable, the implications for policy making are less obvious since the partial derivative depends on the scale on which the rule of law index is measured (1 to 100 in this instance), not to mention the difficulty in deciding what it means—in terms of changing real institutions—to increase rule of law by one point on the scale.

The returns to schooling also depend on other country-specific characteristics. Looking down the columns of table 7.4, the marginal returns to schooling appear to be higher at higher levels of income. This result is attributable to the unobserved characteristics of countries that are captured by the dummy variables in the model. From equation 7.1 it is clear that country-specific characteristics will affect the level of the constant term A. What we are observing in table 7.4 is, in effect, four different functions for intangible capital, one per income group.

Disentangling the Intangible Capital Residual

The Cobb-Douglas specification permits us to go one step further by deriving the following decomposition of the intangible capital residual:

$$R = \frac{\delta R}{\delta S} S + \frac{\delta R}{\delta F} F + \frac{\delta R}{\delta L} L + Z \tag{7.3}$$

The residual can therefore be decomposed into a schooling component, a foreign remittances component, and a governance component. A fourth component, termed Z, captures the difference between intangible capital and the individual contributions of the explanatory variables. In our specification, if the sum of the elasticities α_S, α_F, α_L equals one—which cannot be rejected econometrically—then Z is equal to zero.

Assuming Z equals zero, we can then estimate the contributions of schooling, remittances, and rule of law to the intangible capital residual (figure 7.2). Rule of law is the largest component. On average, it explains 57 percent of the total residual. Schooling is also important with 36 percent of the total value. Foreign remittances account for 7 percent.

A Tale of Three Countries

Three country examples can increase our intuitive understanding of the decomposition of intangible wealth: El Salvador, Peru, and

Figure 7.2 Decomposition of the Intangible Capital Residual, World 2000

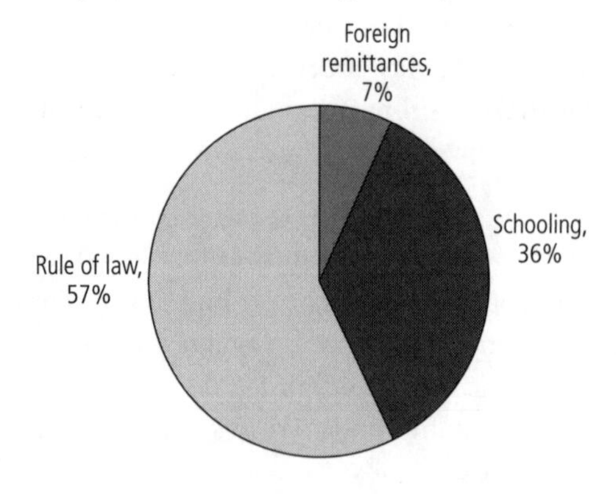

Source: Authors.

Table 7.5 Shares of Residual and Levels of Schooling, Foreign Remittances, and Rule of Law

				Shares of the residual			Levels		
Country	Region	Total wealth ($ per capita)	Intangible capital residual (%)	Schooling (%)	Rule of law (%)	Foreign remittances (%)	Schooling (years per capita)	Rule of law (index)	Foreign remittances ($ per capita)
Turkey	ECA	47,858	75	31	63	6	5	51	68
Peru	LAC	39,045	77	47	51	3	8	39	28
El Salvador	LAC	36,476	86	28	47	24	5	41	284
Lower-middle-income countries		23,612	60	36	57	7	6	44	84

Source: Authors.

Turkey. While enjoying similar levels of total wealth per capita and a very high intangible capital residual, the differences in relative endowments of intangible capital among the three countries are very high. Table 7.5 applies formula 7.3 to decompose the intangible capital residual.

Turkey, located in the Europe and Central Asia region, is the richest of the three countries considered, with a GNI per capita of $2,980. As seen in appendix 2 its total wealth is 18 percent produced capital and 7 percent natural resources (especially agricultural land). Rule of law is the main contributor to a very large intangible capital residual. The rule of law index is above the regional average.

Peru, in Latin America, has a GNI per capita of $1,991. Relatively rich in subsoil resources, Peru has natural capital that accounts for 9 percent of total wealth and a level of produced capital that accounts for 14 percent of wealth (see appendix 2). While rule of law is at a much lower level compared with Turkey, the average school years are higher. As a consequence, schooling explains a large share of the intangible capital residual (47 percent).

El Salvador, located in Central America, yields yet another decomposition of the residual. It has a GNI per capita of $2,075 and a residual that accounts for 86 percent of total wealth. Here remittances play a major role (24 per cent of the residual), reflecting the large share of Salvadoran human capital residing abroad.

The data in table 7.5 suggest that there is no one-size-fits-all policy rule. The varying composition of intangible capital across the three countries suggests very different policy options. In Turkey, education is a major priority. Increasing per capita education in Turkey by one year would raise the residual by nearly 10 percent. In Peru, improving the judicial system to a level similar to Argentina's, for example, would increase the residual by 25 percent.

The management of remittances is a key issue in El Salvador. Adams and Page (2003) show that international remittances have a strong statistical impact on reducing poverty, an impact that could be stronger if policies encouraged investment rather than consumption of remittances. In the long term, increasing the dynamism of the Salvadoran economy would provide an incentive for human capital and financial resources to come back to the country.

Conclusions

Cross-country monetary measures of human capital are not available in the literature. The major impediments to valuing human capital include the availability of data on wages and the comparability of data on education. When available, data are difficult to combine across countries because of differences in definitions, measurement methods, and assumptions. The intangible capital residual obtained from the wealth estimates offers an opportunity for advancing work in this domain.

In addition, while there is a rich literature using governance and institutional indicators as explanatory variables in cross-country growth regressions, there has been little work on trying to place an economic value for issues such as institutional quality. The decomposition of the intangible wealth residual takes some first steps in this direction.

The list of assets that potentially constitute the residual includes human capital, social capital, and the quality of institutions. The regression analysis shows that school years per capita and rule of law account for the largest share of the residual: at the aggregate level, rule of law explains nearly 60 percent of the variation in the residual, while human capital explains another 35 percent.

These results present a plausible menu for development policy. In addition, it is hoped that these results will stimulate new research.

Endnotes

1. If the Russian Federation and Indonesia are excluded from the sample, the correlation coefficient between rule of law and trust becomes 0.73, while the correlation coefficient between control of corruption and trust goes up to 0.70.

2. Statistically speaking, saying that a coefficient is significantly different from zero at the 5 percent level means that there is a 95 percent chance that the coefficient is different from zero.

Chapter 8

Wealth and Production

One of the recurring themes in the sustainability literature has been the legitimacy of using an economic framework to account for natural resources. Those critical of such an approach contend that wealth accounting assumes that produced assets, such as human and physical capital, can substitute for natural-resource assets on a dollar-for-dollar basis. This, they argue, does not capture the limited degree to which such substitution is possible. A loss of some natural capital, such as an entire ecosystem, surely cannot be made up with an increase in physical capital if the very basis of social existence and well-being are destroyed in the areas affected by that system. This makes them skeptical of the kind of wealth accounts we are constructing here.

While we cannot hope to disentangle the full set of issues embedded in this line of reasoning, we can at least start by focusing on the degree of substitutability between the different assets. Underlying any wealth accounts is an implicit *production function,* which is a blueprint of the combinations of different assets with which we can achieve a given level of output. These blueprints are usually written as a mathematical function, which describes the precise relationship between the availability of different amounts of *inputs*, such as physical and human capital services, and the maximum output they could produce. The substitutability between inputs is then measured as an *elasticity of substitution*. In general terms, this captures the ease with which a decline in one input can be compensated by an increase in another, while holding output constant. More precisely, it measures how much the ratio of two inputs (for example, physical capital and land) changes when their relative price changes (for example, the price of land goes up relative to the price of capital).[1] The greater the elasticity, the easier it is to make up for the loss of one resource by using another. Generally, an elasticity of less than one indicates limited substitution possibilities.

A commonly used production function, which implies elasticities of one between the inputs, is the Cobb-Douglas form, written as:

$$Y_t = A_t K^{\alpha} L^{\beta} \tag{8.1}$$

Income or output (Y) is expressed as a function of the levels of capital input (K), labor input (L), an exogenous technological factor (A) and the parameters α and β, which give the returns to capital and labor respectively. If the national production options could be captured by such a function, with natural capital services included, it would have considerable implications for sustainability. First, it would imply a degree of substitutability between natural and produced capital that would give some comfort to those who argue we can lose some natural capital without seriously compromising our well-being. Related to that it would validate the Hartwick rule, which states that when exploiting natural resources, consumption can be sustained at its highest possible level if net saving just equals the rent from exploiting those resources (Hartwick 1977; Hamilton 1995). The Hartwick rule is a useful sustainability policy since it is open to monitoring. We can check whether or not it has been adhered to.

Economists have devoted a considerable amount of effort to estimating these elasticities for inputs such as capital, labor, and energy but *not* natural resources. Although, starting in the 1970s, there were theoretical studies that modeled neoclassical economic growth with nonproduced capital, such as natural resources, as factors in production (Stiglitz 1974a, b; Mitra 1978),[2] the empirical estimation of the underlying production functions was never carried out, largely because of a lack of data.

This chapter is a preliminary attempt in that direction. As mentioned in the earlier chapters, a database of new wealth estimates has been developed, including both produced and nonproduced capital—renewable and nonrenewable resources and human resources—which allows us to estimate a production function that includes the services from these different resources as inputs. This chapter examines, therefore, the economic relationship between total wealth and income generation and takes advantage of the new wealth estimates to estimate a production function based on a larger set of assets. Section 2 presents the estimation of the production function. Section 3 concludes.

Estimation of Nested CES Production Function

The estimation carried out here uses national-level data on gross national income (GNI) or economic output and sees the extent to which variations in GNI across countries, at any point in time, can be explained in terms of the national availability of produced capital, human resources, and natural resources (energy and land resources). A Cobb-Douglas production function of the form shown above is not appropriate for this estimation because it restricts the elasticity between factors to be one. In fact, one of our objectives is to estimate the elasticity of substitution between factors or groups of factors. A form that holds the elasticity constant but allows it to take values different from one is the *constant elasticity of substitution* (CES) production function. In particular, this chapter uses a *nested CES* production function. For example, a two-level nested CES with three inputs takes the form:[3]

$$X = F[X_{AB}(A,B),C] \tag{8.2}$$

where X is the gross output; A, B, and C are inputs; and X_{AB} represents the joint contribution of A and B to production. The first level of the estimation involves A and B; while the second level models the production of output by X_{AB} and C. A special feature of the nested CES function is that the elasticity of substitution between the first-level inputs, A and B, can be different from the elasticity of substitution between the second-level inputs, X_{AB} and C. In other words, by placing natural resources and other inputs in different levels of the function, we effectively allow for different levels of substitutability. So, for example, natural assets may be critical (low substitutability) while other inputs are allowed to be more substitutable among themselves.

There are several studies that have estimated the nested CES production function between three or four production inputs, such as capital, labor, energy, and nonenergy materials at the firm level (Prywes 1986; Manne and Richels 1992; Chang 1994; Kemfert 1998; Kemfert and Welsch 2000). A common interest among these studies is examining the capital-energy substitution in manufacturing industries. For example, Manne and Richels (1992) estimated the substitution possibilities between the capital and labor *nest* and energy to be about 0.4; while Kemfert (1998) estimated the same to be about 0.5. On the other hand, Prywes (1986) found the elasticity of substitution between the capital and energy *nest* and labor to be less than 0.5.

In this chapter we use related variables to estimate aggregate national-level production functions. The variables used are:[4]

- *Produced capital (K)* is an aggregate of equipments, buildings, and urban land.
- *Human capital (H)* has two alternative measures—human capital, which relates educational attainment with labor productivity (*HE*); or intangible capital residual (*HR*), which is obtained as the difference between a country's total wealth and the sum of produced and natural assets. Part of the intangible capital residual captures human capital in the form of raw labor and stock of skills. For further discussion of this variable and its rationale see chapters 2 and 7.
- *Production and net imports of nonrenewable energy resources (E)* includes oil, natural gas, hard coal, and lignite.[5]
- *Land resources (L)* refers to the aggregated value of cropland, pastureland, and protected areas. Land is valued in terms of the present value of the income it generates rather than its market value.

The GNI and all inputs mentioned above are measured in per capita values at 2000 prices and are taken at the national level for 208 countries. GNI data are obtained from the *World Development Indicators* (World Bank 2005). *HE* is derived based on the work by Barro and Lee (2000); *E* is a flow measure and is obtained using the same data that underpin the wealth estimates; while the remaining variables, *K, HR,* and *L* are the components of wealth as described in chapter 2.

The relationships of the production inputs to income are expressed in nested CES production functions described in the chapter annex. Three different nested CES approaches are examined:

- One-level function, with two inputs
- Two-level function, with three inputs
- Three-level function with four inputs

The combinations of the variables in the different CES approaches were varied to further investigate any possible differences among substitution elasticities for pairs of inputs.

The production function approach taken so far neglects an important set of factors that influence differences in national income. These relate to the efficiency with which productive assets are utilized and combined, and include both institutional as well as economic factors. In this study, we consider the following institutional indicators, which capture the efficiency with which production can take place, as well as economic indicators, which also capture the efficiency of economic organization:

- *Institutional development indicators*—indices on voice and accountability (VA), political instability and violence (PIV), government effectiveness (GE), regulatory burden (RB), rule of law (RL); and control of corruption (CC). An increase in a given index measures an improvement in the relevant indicator. Hence, they are expected to have a positive impact on income and possibly growth (Kaufmann and others 2005).[6]

- *Economic indicators*—trade openness (TOPEN) is calculated as the ratio of exports and imports to GDP (World Bank 2005); and the country's domestic credit to the private sector as proportion of GDP (PCREDIT), which represents private sector investments (Beck and others 1999).[7]

Two methods of incorporating the impact of these institutional and economic indicators were investigated. The first method involved the derivation of residuals from the regression of a nested CES production function. The residuals are the part of income not explained by the wealth components—physical capital, human capital, land resources, and energy resources, and are regressed on the identified institutional and economic indicators. By using this method, however, a statistically significant correlation between the residuals and any indicator would imply that relevant variables have been omitted in the estimation of the nested CES production function. Thus, the estimated coefficients of the nested CES production function derived earlier will be biased and inefficient (Greene 2000). Hence another method is considered to be more appropriate. The influences of the institutional and economic indicators on income will be incorporated into the efficiency parameter of the production function, A (see annex 2). Depending on the available data for the variables of the nested CES production function, the number of countries drops in the range of 67 to 93 countries. In the complete case method, for a given nested CES approach, the reduction is caused by considering only those countries that have nonmissing observations for their corresponding dependent and explanatory variables.[8]

Regression Results

The nested CES production functions are estimated using a nonlinear estimation method.[9] The sample size in each CES approach differs because countries with missing observations in any of the variables had to be dropped. Table A8.1.1 in annex 1 shows the estimated substitution elasticities corresponding to the case where human capital is part of the measured intangible capital residual (*HR*). All statistically significant substitution elasticity estimates have a positive sign, which is encouraging.[10] The lowest is that between *K* and *E* at 0.37 in the three-level production function. It is also interesting to note that most of the significant elasticities of substitution are close to one.

A second round of regressions was carried out using the other measure of human capital that is related to schooling and labor productivity, *HE*. Table A8.1.2 in annex 1 shows the statistically significant elasticities of substitution, which also have a positive sign. An elasticity of substitution approximately equal to one is likewise found for most of the nested functions.

The results provide some interesting findings. First, there is no sign that the elasticity of substitution between the natural resource (land) and other inputs is particularly low. Wherever land emerges as a significant input, it has an elasticity of substitution approximately equal to or greater than one. Second, the *HE* variable performs better in the estimation equations than the *HR* variable. Third, the best-determined forms, with all parameters significant, are those using *HE*, involving four factors and containing the combinations:

- *K, HE,* and *L* are nested together and then combine with *E,* or
- *K, HE,* and *E* are nested together and then combine with *L.*

It is hard to distinguish between these two versions, and so they are both used in the further analysis reported below.

From the nested CES production function estimations, the elasticity estimates of the institutional and economic indicators can be derived. Table A8.1.3 and table A8.1.4 in annex 1 show the results for the four-factor production functions [(*K,HE,L*)/*E*] and [(*K,E,HE*)/*L*] of table A8.1.2, respectively. In both tables, the variables on trade openness and private sector investment are found to be statistically significant. The elasticity estimates of these two variables are not very different from each other. The results imply that for every percent increase in trade openness, gross national income per capita (GNIPC) increases by approximately 0.5 percent. None of the institutional indicators, on the other hand, has a statistically significant elasticity estimate.[11]

Simulation

The predicted value of the dependent variable can be calculated by using the estimated coefficient estimates of the production function and the mean values of the explanatory variables. Through this method, we try to predict what will happen to the economic output per capita (GNIPC) if there is significant natural resource depletion. The natural resource considered in this exercise is land resources (L); and the four-factor nested CES production functions used are $[(K,HE,L)/E]$ and $[(K,E,HE)/L]$ of table A8.1.2. Table A8.1.5 in annex 1 presents the predicted average GNIPC, as well as the change in GNIPC given a reduction in the amount of land resources, other things being equal. Based on the production function $[(K,HE,L)/E]$, economic output is reduced by 50 percent when the amount of L declines by about 92 percent, while holding other variables constant. For the production function $[(K,E,HE)/L]$, on the other hand, it takes a reduction in the amount of L by about the same percentage, other things being equal, to halve the economic output relative to the baseline.

Conclusions

In this chapter, we looked at the potential for substituting between different inputs in the generation of GNI. Among these are land resources, one of the most important natural resources. The estimation of a well-known production function form, which allows the elasticities of substitution to be different from one, was carried out. The resulting elasticities involving land resources (between L and other inputs such as physical capital, human capital, and energy resources) were generally around one or greater, which implies a fairly high degree of substitutability. Moreover, it validates the use of a Hartwick rule of saving the rents from the exploitation of natural resources if we are to follow a maximum constant sustainable consumption path.

This result, not surprisingly, has many caveats. Land resources as measured here include cropland, pastureland, and protected areas. Each has been valued in terms of present value of the flow of income that it generates. Such flows, however, underrepresent the importance of, for example, protected areas, which provide significant nonmonetary services, including ecosystem maintenance services that are not included. Further work is needed to include these values, and if this were done, and if the GNI measure were adjusted to allow for these flows of income, the resulting estimates of elasticities of substitution might well change. We intend to continue to work along these lines and to improve the estimates made here.

Another shortcoming of the method applied here is the limited number of factors included in the original estimation. Generating national income depends not on the stock of assets, but on the amounts of the stocks that are used in production and the way in which they are used. For physical and human capital and land, we assume the rate of use is proportional to the stock. That assumption should be improved on, to allow for different utilization rates.

Finally, the chapter also examines how the institutional and economic indicators affect the generation of GNI. Estimation results show that income generation is significantly influenced by changes in trade openness and private sector investment. The institutional indicators, however, have no statistically significant impact on income generation.

Annex 1 Tables

Table A8.1.1 Elasticities of Substitution ($\hat{\sigma}_i$), Using Human Resources (*HR*)

Inputs	Elasticity of substitution $\hat{\sigma}_i$	Elasticity of substitution: Standard error	*R*-squared	Adj. *R*-squared	Sample size
A. Two factors (one-level CES production function)					
(1) *K/HR*	1.00*	3.88E-10	0.9216	0.9131	93
(2) *K/E*	–0.48	2.02	0.9958	0.9951	78
B. Three factors (two-level CES production function)					
(1) *(K,HR)/L*			0.9375	0.9290	93
➢ *K/HR*	6.79	13.92			
➢ *(K,HR)/L*[a]	1.00*	4.33E-10			
(2) *(K,HR)/E*			0.9089	0.8916	70
➢ *K/HR*	–0.78	1.31			
➢ *(K,HR)/E*[a]	1.00*	5.37E-10			
(3) *(K,E)/HR*			0.87667	0.8533	70
➢ *K/E*	0.65	0.69			
➢ *(K,E)/HR*[a]	1.00*	3.96E-09			
C. Four factors (three-level CES production function)					
(1) *(K,HR,L)/E*			0.3435	0.1911	70
➢ *K/HR*	–0.90	0.70			
➢ *(K,HR)/L*[a]	0.97*	0.01			
➢ *(K,HR,L)/E*[b]	1.00*	5.46E-12			
(2) *(K,HR,E)/L*			0.9958	0.9951	78
➢ *K/HR*	–0.13	0.17			
➢ *(K,HR)/E*[a]	0.93*	0.18			
➢ *(K,HR,E)/L*[b]	1.00*	6.52E-09			
(3) *(K,E,HR)/L*			0.9350	0.9200	70
➢ *K/E*	0.37*	0.20			
➢ *(K,E)/HR*[a]	–0.64	0.55			
➢ *(K,E,HR)/L*[b]	1.00*	1.27E-09			

Source: Authors.
Notes:
Legend: *K*=physical capital; *HR*=human capital (captures raw labor and stock of skills); *L*=land resources; *E*=energy resources.
Inputs in parentheses imply that they are nested.
a. Two inputs in a nested function.
b. Three inputs in a nested function.
(*) denotes statistical significance at 5 percent level.
The elasticities of substitution and their corresponding standard errors are rounded off to the nearest hundredth.

Table A8.1.2 Elasticities of Substitution ($\hat{\sigma}_i$), Using Human Capital Related to Schooling (*HE*)

Inputs	Elasticity of substitution		R-squared	Adj. R-squared	Sample size
	$\hat{\sigma}_i$	Standard error			
A. Two factors (one-level CES production function)					
(1) *K/HE*	1.00*	2.50E-08	0.9061	0.8942	81
B. Three factors (two-level CES production function)					
(1) *(K,HE)/L*			0.9203	0.9076	81
➢ *K/HE*	1.01*	0.01			
➢ *(K,HE)/L*[a]	1.00*	2.23E-10			
(2) *(K,HE)/E*			0.8952	0.8742	67
➢ *K/HE*	1.65*	0.12			
➢ *(K,HE)/E*[a]	1.00*	6.76E-11			
(3) *(K,E)/HE*			0.7674	0.7209	67
➢ *K/E*	0.17	0.19			
➢ *(K,E)/HE*[a]	1.00*	8.22E-08			
C. Four factors (three-level CES production function)					
(1) *(K,HE,L)/E*			0.9037	0.8081	67
➢ *K/HE*	1.78*	0.11			
➢ *(K,HE)/L*[a]	1.14*	0.02			
➢ *(K,HE,L)/E*[b]	1.00*	2.52E-12			
(2) *(K,HE,E)/L*			0.9059	0.8828	67
➢ *K/HE*	–8.55	12.61			
➢ *(K,HE)/E*[a]	0.48*	0.17			
➢ *(K,HE,E)/L*[b]	1.00*	4.60E-11			
(3) *(K,E,HE)/L*			0.9062	0.8831	67
➢ *K/E*	1.57*	0.37			
➢ *(K,E)/HE*[a]	0.92*	0.02			
➢ *(K,E,HE)/L*[b]	1.00*	6.41E-11			

Source: Authors.

Notes:

Legend: *K*=physical capital; *HE*=human capital related to educational attainment and labor productivity; *L*=land resources; *E*=energy resources.

Inputs in parentheses imply that they are nested.

a. Two inputs in a nested function.

b. Three inputs in a nested function.

(*) denotes statistical significance at 5 percent level; (**) at 10 percent level.

The elasticities of subtitution and their corresponding standard errors are rounded off to the nearest hundredth.

Table A8.1.3 Elasticity Estimates of the Economic and Institutional Indicators, Using the [(*K, HE, L*)/*E*] Production Function

Variable	Elasticity	Standard error	*t*-statistic
TOPEN	0.47	0.10	4.53
PCREDIT	0.51	0.12	4.25
VA	0.01	0.04	0.28
PIV	–0.01	0.02	–0.28
GE	0.04	0.10	0.40
RB	0.03	0.07	0.39
RL	–0.07	0.10	–0.73
CC	0.01	0.09	0.17

Source: Authors.
Note: Legend: *TOPEN*=trade openness; *PCREDIT*=variable for private sector investment; *VA*=voice and accountability; *PIV*=political instability and violence; *GE*=government effectiveness; *RB*=regulatory burden; *RL*= rule of law; and *CC*=control of corruption.

Table A8.1.4 Elasticity Estimates of the Economic and Institutional Indicators, Using the [(*K, E, HE*)/*L*] Production Function

Variable	Elasticity	Standard error	*t*-statistic
TOPEN	0.50	0.09	5.27
PCREDIT	0.51	0.11	4.83
VA	0.02	0.03	0.45
PIV	–0.01	0.02	–0.44
GE	0.06	0.09	0.62
RB	0.03	0.07	0.37
RL	–0.08	0.09	–0.86
CC	–0.02	0.08	–0.24

Source: Authors.
Note: Legend: *TOPEN*=trade openness; *PCREDIT*=variable for private sector investment; *VA*=voice and accountability; *PIV*=political instability and violence; *GE*=government effectiveness; *RB*=regulatory burden; *RL*=rule of law; and *CC*=control of corruption.

Table A8.1.5 Level of Gross National Income per Capita, Given a Reduction in the Amount of Land

		Reduction in the amount of land by			
Prod. function	Baseline*	20%	50%	75%	92%
(K,HE,L)/E	$8,638.10	$8,068.84	$7,019.27	$5,774.25	$4,297.16
*Difference from baseline***		*(–7%)*	*(–19%)*	*(–33%)*	*(–50%)*
(K,E,HE)/L	$9,096.20	$8,540.27	$7,477.97	$6,147.62	$4,455.06
*Difference from baseline***		*(–6%)*	*(–18%)*	*(–32%)*	*(–51%)*

Source: Authors.
Notes:
*Predicted per capita GNI at the mean values of the explanatory variables.
**Rounded off to the nearest whole number.
Sample size of each production function = 67.

Annex 2 Three Different CES Approaches

1. A traditional CES production function with two inputs is written as:

(a) Physical capital *(K)* and human capital *(H)*

$$Y = A\left(aK^{-\beta} + bH^{-\beta}\right)^{-1/\beta} \tag{A.1}$$

(b) Physical capital *(K)* and energy resources *(E)*

$$Y = A(aK^{-\beta} + bE^{-\beta})^{-1/\beta} \tag{A.2}$$

where Y is the per capita gross national income. A is an efficiency parameter. a and b are distribution parameters that lie between zero and one and β represents the substitution parameter. The elasticity of substitution (σ) is calculated as: $\sigma = (1/[1+\beta])$. Values of β must be greater than –1 (a value less than –1 is economically nonsensical, although it has been observed in a number of studies [Prywes 1986]). If $\beta > -1$, the elasticity of substitution must, of course, be positive.

A, the efficiency parameter, is assumed to be a function of the economic (*TOPEN* and *PCREDIT*) and institutional indicators described in the text. Two functional forms of A have been tried:

(c) $$A = e^{\lambda_1 TOPEN + \lambda_2 PCREDIT + \lambda_3 VA + \lambda_4 PIV + \lambda_5 GE + \lambda_6 RB + \lambda_7 RL + \lambda_8 CC} \tag{A.3}$$

(d) $$A = \lambda_1 TOPEN + \lambda_2 PCREDIT + \lambda_3 VA + \lambda_4 PIV + \lambda_5 GE + \lambda_6 RB + \lambda_7 RL + \lambda_8 CC \tag{A.4}$$

and the second functional form of A was found to be more appropriate.

TOPEN means trade openness; *PCREDIT* is a variable for private sector investment; *VA*, voice and accountability; *PIV*, political instability and violence; *GE*, government effectiveness; *RB*, regulatory burden; *RL*, rule of law; and *CC*, control of corruption. The scores for each institutional indicator lie between –2.5 and 2.5, with higher scores corresponding to better outcomes.

2. A two-level nested CES production function with three inputs is investigated for three cases:

(a) K and H in the nested function, X_{KH} is a substitute for land resources (L):

$$Y_1 = A_1\left[a_1\left(b_1K^{-\alpha_1} + (1-b_1)H^{-\alpha_1}\right)^{\beta_1/\alpha_1} + (1-a_1)L^{-\beta_1}\right]^{-1/\beta_1} \tag{A.5}$$

(b) K and H in the nested function, X_{KH} is a substitute for energy resources (E):

$$Y_2 = A_2\left[a_2\left(b_2K^{-\alpha_2} + (1-b_2)H^{-\alpha_2}\right)^{\beta_2/\alpha_2} + (1-a_2)E^{-\beta_2}\right]^{-1/\beta_2} \quad (A.6)$$

(c) K and E in the nested function, X_{KE} is a substitute for human capital (H):

$$Y_3 = A_3\left[a_3\left(b_3K^{-\alpha_3} + (1-b_3)E^{-\alpha_3}\right)^{\beta_3/\alpha_3} + (1-a_3)H^{-\beta_3}\right]^{-1/\beta_3} \quad (A.7)$$

where α_i and β_i are substitution parameters.

3. A three-level nested CES production function with four inputs is studied for these three cases:

(a) K, H, and L in the nested function, and E as a substitute for X_{KHL}:

$$Y_4 = A_4\left\{a_4\left[b_4\left(c_4K^{-\alpha_4} + (1-c_4)H^{-\alpha_4}\right)^{\rho_4/\alpha_4} + (1-b_4)L^{-\rho_4}\right]^{\beta_4/\rho_4} + (1-a_4)E^{-\beta_4}\right\}^{-1/\beta_4} \quad (A.8)$$

(b) P, H, and E in the nested function, and L as a substitute for X_{KHE}:

$$Y_5 = A_5\left\{a_5\left[b_5\left(c_5K^{-\alpha_5} + (1-c_5)H^{-\alpha_5}\right)^{\rho_5/\alpha_5} + (1-b_5)E^{-\rho_5}\right]^{\beta_5/\rho_5} + (1-a_5)L^{-\beta_5}\right\}^{-1/\beta_5} \quad (A.9)$$

(c) K, E, and H in the nested function, and L as a substitute for X_{KEH}:

$$Y_6 = A_6\left\{a_6\left[b_6\left(c_6K^{-\alpha_6} + (1-c_6)E^{-\alpha_6}\right)^{\rho_6/\alpha_6} + (1-b_6)H^{-\rho_6}\right]^{\beta_6/\rho_6} + (1-a_6)L_6^{-\beta_6}\right\}^{-1/\beta_6} \quad (A.10)$$

where α_i, ρ_i, β_i are substitution parameters; and $0 < a_i, b_i, c_i < 1$.

The substitution elasticities for these CES approaches can be described as follows:

$\sigma_{\alpha_i} = 1/1+\alpha_i$	Gives the elasticity of substitution between K and H when $i = 1,2,4,5$ Gives the elasticity of substitution between K and E when $i = 1,6$
$\sigma_{\rho_i} = 1/1+\rho_i$	Gives the elasticity of substitution between K/H and L when $i = 4$ Gives the elasticity of substitution between K/H and E when $i = 5$ Gives the elasticity of substitution between K/E and H when $i = 6$
$\sigma_{\beta_i} = 1/1+\beta_i$	Gives the elasticity of substitution between K/H and L when $i = 1$ Gives the elasticity of substitution between K/H and E when $i = 2$ Gives the elasticity of substitution between K/E and H when $i = 3$ Gives the elasticity of substitution between $K/H/L$ and E when $i = 4$ Gives the elasticity of substitution between $K/H/E$ and L when $i = 5$ Gives the elasticity of substitution between $K/E/H$ and L when $i = 6$

The nested CES production functions are estimated using the nonlinear estimation method via the STATA program. The nonlinear estimation program uses an iterative procedure to find the parameter values in the relationship that cause the sum of squared residuals (SSR) to be minimized. It starts with approximate guesses of the parameter values (also called *starting values*), and computes the residuals and then the SSR. The starting values are a combination of arbitrary values and coefficient estimates of a nested CES production function. For example, the starting values of equation (A.1) are arbitrary. A set of numbers is tried until convergence is achieved. On the other hand, the starting values of equation (A.5) are based on the coefficient estimates of equation (A.1). Next, it changes one of the parameter values slightly and computes again the residuals to see whether the SSR becomes smaller or larger. The iteration process goes on until there is convergence—it finds parameter values that, when changed slightly in any direction, cause the SSR to rise. Hence, these parameter values are the least squares estimate in the nonlinear context.

Endnotes

1. Where prices are not defined, we measure the change in the ratio of the inputs resulting from a change in the marginal rate at which one factor can be substituted for another (Chiang 1984).

2. A bibliographical compilation of studies can be found in Wagner (2004). One exception to the observation that there is little empirical work is Berndt and Field (1981), who did look at limited natural resource substitution between capital, labor, energy, and materials. The studies generally found low elasticities between capital and materials. They did not, however, look at land as an input in the way we do here. Nor did they work with national-level data.

3. This model makes the further assumption of *homothetic weak separability* for groups of inputs. *Homothetic weak separability* means that the marginal rate of substitution between inputs in a certain group is independent of output and of the level of inputs outside that group (Chiang 1984).

4. Per capita dollar values at nominal 2000 prices are used.

5. For energy it would be inappropriate to take the stock value of the asset, as what is relevant for production is the flow of energy available to the economy. This is given by production plus net imports. With the other assets (K, H, and L) it is also the flow that matters, but it is more reasonable to assume that the flow is proportional to the stock. We do note, however, in the conclusions that even this assumption needs to be changed in future work.

6. Data can be obtained from the website: *http://www.worldbank.org/wbi/governance/pubs/govmatters4.html.*

7. Hnatkovska and Loayza (2004) use openness and credit as a measure of financial depth, which they find to have a positive impact on growth. Data for this indicator can be obtained from the following website: *http://www.worldbank.org/research/projects/finstructure/database.htm.*

8. An *imputation method* was tried to fill the missing values for some of the countries to keep all 208 countries in the estimation. Most of the results, however, were not found to be reasonable. For example, the imputed value of physical capital for a low-income country turned out to be too high compared with the average value of physical capital of its income group. Hence, the imputation method was not used since it poses more problems in the estimates than using the *complete case method.*

9. See annex 2 for more details.

10. A negative elasticity of substitution is economically nonsensical—it implies a decline in the availability of one input can be *made up* by a decline in the availability of other factors. Nevertheless, some production function studies do find such negative values.

11. In the regression where the residuals are expressed as a function of the institutional variables, we did find significant values for a few institutional variables, especially the rule of law, which was encouraging as that variable also emerges as important in other evaluations of intercountry differences in this study. Unfortunately, the result did not hold when the more appropriate method was used.

PART 4

INTERNATIONAL EXPERIENCE

Chapter 9

Developing and Using Environmental Accounts

Having committed themselves to achieving sustainable development, governments face a number of challenges beyond the traditional concerns of their natural resources and environmental agencies. One of the most important of these is integrating economic policies with policies for the management of natural resources and the environment. Policy makers setting environmental standards need to be aware of the likely consequences for the economy, while economic policy makers must consider the sustainability of current and projected patterns of production and consumption.

Such integration and adoption of the notion of sustainable development by governments have been the motivation for developing environmental accounting. Environmental accounts can provide policy makers with the following:

- Indicators and descriptive statistics to monitor the interaction between the environment and the economy, and progress toward meeting environment goals
- A quantitative basis for strategic planning and policy analysis to identify more sustainable development paths and the appropriate policy instruments for achieving these paths

After providing a context to explore the usefulness of the system of integrated environmental and economic accounting (SEEA) as an operational framework for monitoring sustainability and its policy use, this chapter summarizes the four general components of the environmental accounts.[1] The second part of the chapter reviews a few policy applications of economic accounting (EA) in industrialized and developing countries and indicates potential applications, which may not be fully exploited at this time.

Developing the Environmental Account: A Bird's Eye View

Environmental and resource accounting has evolved since the 1970s through the efforts of individual countries or practitioners, developing their own frameworks and methodologies to represent their environmental priorities. Since the early 1990s, the United Nations Statistics Division, the European Union (EU), the Organisation for Economic Co-operation and Development (OECD), the World Bank, in-country statistical offices, and other organizations have made a concerted effort to standardize the framework and methodologies. The United Nations (UN) published an interim handbook on environmental accounting in 1993 (UN 1993), as well as an operational handbook (UN 2000). The former was revised as *Integrated Environmental and Economic Accounting 2003* (SEEA). The discussion below describes the different methodologies and how they are related to the revised SEEA.

Environmental accounts have four main components:

- Natural resource asset accounts, which deal mainly with stocks of natural resources and focus on revising the balance sheets of the system of national accounts (SNA).
- Pollutant and material (energy and resources) flow accounts, which provide information at the industry level about the use of energy and materials as inputs to production and final demand, and the generation of pollutants and solid waste. These accounts are linked to the supply and use tables of the SNA, which are used to construct input-output (IO) tables.
- Environmental protection and resource management expenditures, which identify expenditures in the conventional SNA incurred by industry, government, and households to protect the environment or manage resources.
- Environmentally adjusted macroeconomic aggregates, which include indicators of sustainability such as the environmentally adjusted net domestic product (eaNDP).

Environmental Accounts and Concepts of Sustainability

As discussed in earlier chapters, many of the concerns about resource depletion and environmental degradation are reflected in the concept of sustainable development, defined as "... development that meets the needs of the present without compromising the ability of future generations to meet their own needs" (World Commission on Environment and Development 1987). Consistent with Hicks's notion of income (Hicks 1946), sustainability requires nondecreasing levels of capital stock over time or, at the level of the individual, nondecreasing per capita capital stock. Indicators of sustainability could be based on either the value of total assets every period, or by the change in wealth and the consumption of capital (depreciation) in the conventional national accounts.

Economic sustainability can be defined as *strong* or *weak,* reflecting controversy over the degree to which one form of capital can substitute for another. Weak sustainability requires only that the combined *value* of all assets remain constant. Strong sustainability is based on the concept that natural capital is a complement to manufactured capital, rather than a substitute. An indicator of strong sustainability, therefore, requires that all natural capital is measured in physical units. A less extreme version of strong sustainability accepts some degree of substitutability among assets, but recognizes that there are some *critical* assets which are irreplaceable. The corresponding measure of sustainability would be partly monetary (for those assets, manufactured and natural, which are not critical and for which substitution is allowed) and partly physical, for natural assets which are critical.

Asset Accounts

Natural resource asset accounts follow the structure of the asset accounts of the SNA, with data for opening stocks, closing stocks, and changes during the year. The changes that occur during the period are divided into those that are the result of economic activity (for example, extraction of minerals or harvesting of forests) and those that are the result of natural processes (for example, growth, births, and deaths). There is some controversy over how to treat new discoveries of minerals: as an economic change (the result of exploration activities) or as part of other volume changes. The monetary accounts for resources have an additional component, like manufactured capital, for revaluation.

Measurement of the physical stocks can present problems both as to what to measure as well as how to measure. In some earlier versions of subsoil (mineral) asset accounts, only economically proven stocks were included in the asset accounts. Some countries have modified this to include a portion of probable and possible stocks, based on the probability of these stocks becoming economically feasible to mine. Certain resources, like marine-capture fisheries, are not observed directly and require biological models to estimate stocks and changes in stocks.

Two methods have been used to value assets: net present value (NPV) and net price (this is just equal to the total resource rent per unit of resource). The NPV method of valuation requires assumptions about future prices and costs of extraction, the rate of extraction, and the discount rate. It is often assumed that net price and level of extraction remain constant, although when information is known about planned extraction paths or expected future prices, this information can be incorporated. A wide range of discount rates have been used by different countries.

In much of the early work on environmental accounting (Repetto and others 1989; Bartelmus and others 1992; van Tongeren and others 1991; UN 1993), the net-price method rather than NPV was used to value assets. The net-price method simply applies the net price in a given year to the entire remaining stock. The revised SEEA recommends NPV, and this method has become more widely used than the net-price method in more recent work.

Pollution and Material Flow Accounts

Pollution and material (including energy and resource) flow accounts track the use of materials and energy and the generation of pollution by each industry and final demand sector. The flows are linked through the use of a common industrial and commodity classification to IO tables and social accounting matrices (SAMs), as exemplified by the Dutch national accounting matrix, including the environmental accounts (NAMEA) framework, which has been adopted by Eurostat (the European Commission's official statistical agency) and the revised SEEA manual. Much of the work on environmental accounts has been pioneered by industrialized countries and reflects their major policy concerns.

Physical Accounts

The most widely available accounts are for energy and air emissions, especially emissions linked to the use of fossil fuels. Energy accounts have been constructed by many countries since the dramatic oil-price increases of the 1970s, and because many air pollutants are linked to energy use, it is relatively simple to extend the accounts to include these pollutants. Transboundary flows of atmospheric pollutants that cause acid rain have been a major policy concern throughout Europe for more than two decades. More recently, the concern with climate change has made tracking greenhouse gas emissions a priority. Accounts are also constructed for other air pollutants, water pollutants, solid waste, and other forms of environmental degradation such as soil erosion. In a growing number of countries, especially water-scarce countries (Australia, Botswana, Chile, France, Moldova, Namibia, and Spain), water accounts are a high priority.

Monetary Accounts for Environmental Degradation

In many countries, assigning an economic value to environmental benefits and damage may be considered the most effective way to influence policy, if not the most efficient way to design policy. However, controversy remains over whether these monetary estimates are properly part of the environmental accounts or a separate analysis of the (physical) accounts. Nevertheless, most countries attempt some valuation using one of two different approaches to valuation (or sometimes both, for comparison):

- Maintenance, or avoidance cost approach, which measures the cost of measures to reduce pollution to a given standard
- Damage cost approach, which measures the actual damage caused by pollution in, for example, reduced agricultural productivity resulting from soil erosion, increased corrosion of structures from acid rain, or damage to human health from water pollution

Willingness to pay can be used to value damage costs, although it is not widely used in environmental accounting efforts by countries at this time. Measuring damages caused by pollution is difficult—although it is theoretically the best method to deal with pollution in the accounts, it has not been used as often as the maintenance cost approach.

Monetary Accounts for Nonmarketed Resources

Valuation issues discussed in the SEEA have largely focused on environmental degradation, but other nonmarket goods and services also need to be valued. The use of near-market goods like nonmarket firewood or wild-food products are, in principle, included in the SNA, and many countries have included some estimate of these resources in the conventional national accounts. Water, on the other hand, is an example of an economically important resource that is often either not priced or priced in a way that is not related to its true economic value.

Environmental Protection and Resource Management Accounts

This third component of the SEEA differs from the others in that it does not add any new information to the national accounts, but reorganizes expenditures in the conventional SNA that are closely related to environmental protection and resource management. The purpose is to make these expenditures more explicit, and thus more useful for policy analysis. In this sense, they are similar to other satellite accounts, such as transportation or tourism accounts, which do not necessarily add new information, but reorganize existing information. This set of accounts has three quite distinct components:

- Expenditures for environmental protection and resource management, by public and private sectors
- The activities of industries that provide environmental protection services
- Environmental and resource taxes or subsidies

The environmental protection expenditure (EPE) represents part of society's effort to prevent or to reduce pressures on the environment, but the interpretation of indicators from the EPE accounts can be ambiguous. The EPE concept works best for end-of-pipe, pollution-abatement technologies in which an additional production cost is incurred to reduce pollution. The growing trend in pollution management stresses pollution prevention through redesign of industrial processes rather than end-of-pipe technology. New technology may be introduced, perhaps during the normal course of replacement and expansion of capacity that reduces pollution. However, no consensus exists about what share to attribute to the EPE. In some instances, process-integrated measures that reduce pollution may reduce costs and pollution simultaneously. The EU is responding to this problem by collecting data about the use of integrated-process technologies. Surveys of recycling are also included.

Macroeconomic Indicators

Each of the three sets of accounts considered so far provides a range of indicators, but, with the exception of the asset accounts, these indicators do not directly affect the conventional macroeconomic indicators such as gross domestic product (GDP) and net domestic product (NDP). Many practitioners have searched for a way to measure sustainability by revising conventional macroeconomic indicators or by producing alternative macroindicators in physical units.

Physical Indicators

Macroeconomic indicators measured in physical units have been proposed either as an alternative to monetary indicators or to be used in conjunction with monetary aggregates in assessing economic performance. Physical indicators reflect a strong sustainability approach. The two major sources of physical macroeconomic indicators are the NAMEA component of the SEEA flow accounts and material flow accounts (MFA), which are closely related to environmental accounts.

The NAMEA provides physical macroeconomic indicators for major environmental policy themes: climate change, acidification of the atmosphere, eutrophication of water bodies, and solid waste. These indicators are compiled by aggregating related emissions using some common measurement unit, such as carbon dioxide equivalents for greenhouse gases. The indicators are then compared with a national standard—such as the target level of greenhouse-gas emissions—to assess sustainability. The NAMEA does not, however, provide a single-valued indicator which aggregates across all themes.

The MFA provide several macroindicators; the most widely known is total material requirements (TMR) (Bartelmus and Vesper 2000; World Resources Institute 2000). TMR sums all the material use in an economy by weight, including *hidden flows,* which consist of materials excavated or disturbed along with the desired material, but which do not themselves enter the economy. In contrast to NAMEA theme indicators, TMR provides a single-valued indicator for all material use.

Monetary Indicators

The purpose of most monetary environmental macroeconomic aggregates has been to provide a more accurate measure of sustainable income. The first approach revised conventional macroeconomic indicators by adding and subtracting the relevant environmental components from the SEEA, the depletion of natural capital, and environmental degradation (O'Connor 2000). Most economists and statisticians accept the adjustment of NDP for asset depletion, in principle, even though there is not yet a consensus over the correct way to measure it. However, some economists and statisticians have criticized environmentally adjusted NDP (eaNDP) for combining actual transactions (conventional NDP) with hypothetical values (monetary value of environmental degradation). If the costs of environmental mitigation had actually been paid, relative prices throughout the economy would have changed, thereby affecting economic behavior and, ultimately, the level and structure of GDP and NDP.

A macroindicator related to eaNDP is adjusted net saving (genuine saving), which is reported in the World Bank's annual *World Development Indicators* (Kunte and others 1998; Hamilton 2000; World Bank 2005), and discussed earlier in detail in chapter 3. The criticism of eaNDP led to the construction of a second approach to constructing indicators, which asks the question, what would the GDP or NDP have been if the economy were required to meet sustainability standards? These indicators of a hypothetical economy are derived through economic modeling. Two modeling approaches were developed:

- Hueting's sustainable national income (SNI), which estimates what the level of national income would be if the economy met all environmental standards using currently available technology (Verbruggen and others 2000)
- Greened economy NDP (geNDP), which estimates how the economy would respond if the estimated maintenance costs were internalized in the economy

International Experience

Several countries construct environmental accounts on a regular basis with various levels of coverage, employing one or more of the above approaches. Table 9.1 identifies the major countries that are constructing

Table 9.1 Countries with Environmental Accounting Programs

		Flow accounts for pollutants & materials		Environmental protection & resource management expenditures	Macro-aggregates
	Assets	Physical	Monetary		
Industrialized countries					
Australia	X	X		X	
Canada	X	X		X	
Denmark	X	X		X	
Finland	X	X		X	
France	X	X		X	
Germany	X	X	X	X	X
Italy	X	X		X	
Japan	X	X	X	X	X
Norway	X	X			
Sweden	X	X	X	X	X
United Kingdom	X	X		X	
United States	X			X	
Developing countries					
Botswana	X	X	X[a]		
Chile	X		X[a]	X	
Korea, Rep. of	X	X	X	X	X
Mexico	X	X	X	X	X
Moldova		X[a]			
Namibia	X	X	X[a]		
Philippines	X	X	X	X	X
Occasional studies					
Colombia		X	X	X	
Costa Rica				X	
EU-15			X		
Indonesia	X				
South Africa	X	X	X[a]		

Source: Authors.
Note: Other European countries have also constructed environmental accounts but are not included here because of the limited policy analysis of the accounts. EU-15: European Union.
a. Accounts for water only.

EA on an ongoing basis in their statistical offices or other government ministries. Most of the work is being done in Australia, Canada, Europe, and a few developing countries. Of the developing countries, Botswana, Namibia, and the Philippines are particularly important because policy analysis was built into the EA project design. There are countless other one-time or academic studies, a few of which are referred to in the second part of this chapter.

Applications and Policy Uses of the SEEA

Broadly speaking, there are two sorts of applications of environmental accounting. The first is closest to statistical tradition and concerns the development of indicators and descriptive statistics of the various subject areas. The second shows how specific policy analyses can be based on the techniques provided by SEEA. Policy analysis usually requires more specialized expertise in the techniques of economic analysis and modeling, which may be lacking in some statistical offices.

Use of Asset Accounts for Monitoring and Policy Making

One of the fundamental indicators of a country's well-being is the value of its wealth over time. The discussion of sustainability indicated that there are different views about how wealth should be measured, that is, whether all forms of wealth can be measured in monetary terms (weak sustainability) or in some combination of monetary and physical units (strong sustainability). Asset accounts can contribute to more effective monitoring of national wealth. They can also be used to improve management of natural capital.

Monitoring Total Wealth and Changes in Natural Capital

The asset accounts provide fundamental indicators to monitor sustainability—the value of wealth and how it changes from one period to the next through depreciation or accumulation. Although total wealth and per capita wealth, expanded to include both manufactured and natural assets, are useful indicators, not many countries compile such figures yet. Instead, many countries have focused on compiling accounts for individual resources, sometimes estimating depletion of natural capital, which is used to compile a more comprehensive measure of depreciation than is found in the conventional national accounts

Physical asset accounts. The physical asset accounts provide indicators of ecological sustainability and detailed information for the management of resources. The volume of mineral reserves, for example, is needed to plan extraction paths and indicates how long a country can rely on its minerals. The volume of fish or forestry biomass, especially when disaggregated by age class, helps to determine sustainable yields and the harvesting policies appropriate to that yield.

The asset accounts track the changes in stock over time and indicate whether depletion is occurring. Thus, they can show the effects of resource policy on the stock and can be used to motivate a change in policy. For example, the biological depletion of Namibia's fish stocks since the 1960s has provided a very clear picture to policy makers of the devastating impact of uncontrolled, open-access fishing (figure 9.1). Similar accounts of depletion (or accumulation) have been constructed for forests in Australia, Brazil, Canada, Chile, Indonesia, Malaysia, the Philippines, and much of the EU.

Figure 9.1 Biomass of Hake, Pilchard, Horse Mackerel in Namibia, 1963–1999

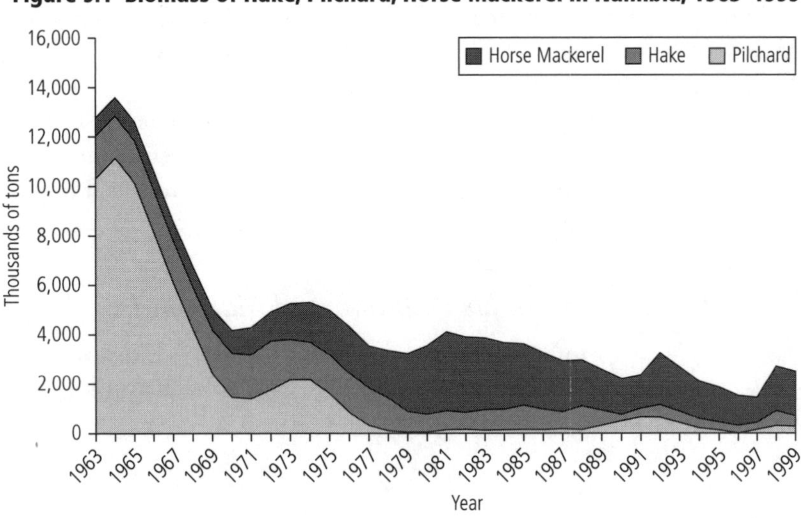

Source: Lange 2003a.

Monetary asset accounts. The physical accounts for individual assets can be used to monitor ecological sustainability. However, the economic value of a resource must also be known for a more complete assessment. The monetary value of different assets, produced and nonproduced, can be combined to provide a figure for total national wealth. This figure can be analyzed to assess the diversity of wealth, its ownership distribution, and its volatility resulting from price fluctuations, an important feature for economies dependent on primary commodities.

Most countries with asset accounts for natural capital have typically published the accounts separately for each resource and have not attempted to measure total natural capital (the sum of all resources) total national wealth (the sum of manufactured and natural capital). Among developing countries, Botswana (Lange 2000a) and Namibia (Lange 2003a) are doing so. Among the industrialized countries, Australia (Australian Bureau of Statistics 1999) and Canada (Statistics Canada 2000) have integrated nonproduced natural assets with produced assets in their balance sheets.

Managing Resources: Economic Efficiency and Sustainability

In the early days of environmental accounting, resource rent was calculated in order to calculate the value of assets, but its usefulness as a resource management tool was not always recognized. The work by Norway (Sorenson and Hass 1998), Eurostat (2000) for subsoil assets, in the Philippines Environment and Natural Resource Accounting Project [ENRAP] 1999; Lange 2000b, Botswana (Lange 2000a), Namibia (Lange and Motinga 1997; Lange 2003a), and in South Africa (Blignaut and others 2000) has included detailed analysis of resource rent. Rent has been used to assess resource management in terms of economic efficiency, sustainability, and other socioeconomic objectives, such as intergenerational equity.

Physical Flow Accounts for Pollution and Material Use

Data from the physical flow accounts are used to assess pressure on the environment and to evaluate alternative options for reducing pressure on the environment.

Physical Flow Accounts

At their simplest, the flow accounts monitor the time trend of resource use, pollution emissions, and environmental degradation, both by industry and in aggregate. A rising level of emissions, for example, would be a clear warning sign of environmental problems.

The overview of environmental trends helps assess whether national goals, typically set in terms of total figures for emissions or material use, are being achieved. A great deal of work has been done throughout the industrialized world to construct time series of pollution emissions and energy use. Similar work has been done for water accounts by a number of countries, including Botswana, Chile, France, Moldova, Namibia, the Philippines, South Africa, and Spain. The example for Botswana shows declining per capita water use and declining water intensity of the economy (measured by the GDP per cubic meter of water used), but the volume of water has still increased because population and GDP growth outweigh the gains in efficiency (table 9.2).

Table 9.2 Index of Water Use, GDP Growth, and Population Growth in Botswana, 1993 to 1999 (1993 = 1.00)

	1993/94	1994/95	1995/96	1996/97	1997/98	1998/99
Volume of water used	1.00	1.01	1.03	0.99	1.04	1.05
Per capita water use	1.00	0.99	0.98	0.92	0.94	0.93
GDP per m^3 water used	1.00	1.02	1.06	1.18	1.22	1.26

Source: Lange and others 2000.
Note: m^3 = cubic meter

Policy Analysis

The flow accounts are widely used for policy analysis, for example, to assess the impact of environmental tax reform, to design economic instruments to reduce pollution emissions, and to assess competitiveness under new, more restrictive environmental policies. The EU has been the largest user of the accounts and has used them mainly to address two priorities: greenhouse gas emissions and acid rain.

Norway has used the flow accounts for energy and greenhouse gas emissions to assess a policy that many countries are considering: changing the structure of taxes to increase taxes on emissions and resource use, while simultaneously reducing other taxes by an equal amount in order to remain fiscally neutral, the so-called "*double dividend.*" Norway used its multisector, general-equilibrium model to look specifically at increasing the carbon tax to NKr 700 per ton of carbon dioxide with a compensating decrease in its payroll tax. Policy makers in Norway wanted to know what effects this tax reform would have on economic welfare. Using the general-equilibrium model, Norway initially found that employment and economic welfare would increase while carbon emissions declined. However, closer analysis of the results indicated that the tax reform would result in significant structural change in the economy—certain energy-intensive industries in the metal, chemical, and oil-refining sectors were particularly hard hit by the tax, and would reduce output and employment considerably.

Environmental Protection and Resource Management Accounts

This set of accounts has several quite distinct components, including:

- Expenditures for environmental protection and resource management, by public and private sectors
- Activities of industries that provide environmental protection services
- Environmental and resource taxes or subsidies

Environmental Protection Expenditure Accounts

Of the three components of this part of the accounts, EPE accounts have been the most widely constructed, mainly in the United States, Canada, the EU, Japan, and Australia. Some developing countries have also constructed EPE accounts, notably Chile, Colombia, the Republic of Korea, and the Philippines. Eurostat has published a handbook with a detailed list of indicators that can be obtained from the EPE accounts, from the most general (for example, time trend of EPE by sector and domain) to detailed (for example, spending within industries by domain). EPE accounts for the United States, for example, show that, as a percentage of GDP, expenditures have remained constant between 1.7 and 1.8 percent. Of the four developing countries that have compiled EPE, coverage differs from country to country. Only Colombia and the Republic of Korea cover EPE by all sectors. Costa Rica and the Philippines have compiled only EPE by government.

Environmental Services Industry

While EPE accounts have imposed substantial costs, they have also created opportunities: entirely new industries have arisen to fill the need for environmental services. The second part of the EPE accounts provides a clear definition of environmental services as well as the environmental services industry's contribution to GDP, employment, and exports. For some countries, the environmental services industry has become an important exporter, while other countries are large importers of these services. For example, in France, the environmental services industry accounted for 2.3 percent of GDP and 1.4 percent of employment in 1997. More than half the employment was in solid waste and wastewater management (Desaulty and Templé 1999).

Environmental and Resource Taxes

The third part of the EPE accounts includes taxes and other fees collected by government for pollution emissions and for resource use, such as levies on minerals, forestry, or fisheries. Environmental taxes and subsidies are important policy instruments for achieving sustainability. Many European countries are exploring the possibility of substituting green taxes for other forms of taxes to achieve a *double dividend.* The tax component of the EPE account can be very useful in assessing whether the tax regime provides incentives or disincentives for sustainable development, and whether taxes truly reflect the *polluter pays* principle that many countries have adopted. Taxes on specific natural resources and their use in resource management were discussed in the section on asset accounts.

Economywide Indicators of Sustainable Development

Many practitioners have searched for a way to measure sustainability either by revising conventional macroindicators or by producing new ones in physical units. Aggregate environmental theme indicators measured in physical units are derived from the NAMEA component of the SEEA. The physical indicators are meant to be used in conjunction with conventional economic indicators to assess environmental health and economic progress. A number of different revised environmental monetary aggregates have been calculated by different countries; all are discussed in the revised SEEA. At this time, there is no consensus over which indicators to use. Because each indicator serves a somewhat different policy purpose, the choice of indicator depends on the policy question.

Physical Indicators of Macrolevel Performance

The NAMEA provides physical macroeconomic indicators for major environmental policy themes: climate change, acidification of the atmosphere, eutrophication of water bodies, and solid waste. The indicators can be compared with a national standard—such as the target level of greenhouse-gas emissions—to assess sustainability. A national standard for greenhouse-gas emissions set, for example, in terms of a country's target under the Kyoto Protocol, can be useful. It may not be easy to assess some themes, such as eutrophication, which may have a more local impact, against a national standard. The NAMEA does not provide a single-valued indicator which aggregates across all themes.

The material-flow accounts provide another set of physical macroeconomic indicators, of which the most widely known is TMR. The TMR sums all the material use in an economy by weight. Its purpose, like the monetary aggregates, is to provide a single-valued indicator to measure dematerialization—the decoupling of economic growth from material use.

The World Resources Institute study of MFA for five industrialized countries finds significant decoupling: since 1975, the material intensity of GDP in all five countries has declined by 20 to 40 percent (figure 9.2). This has been the result of efforts to reduce the volume of solid waste and the shift away from energy- and material-intensive industries toward knowledge-based and service industries. Per capita material intensity has not declined in most countries over this time period. Only Germany showed a decline of 6 percent.

Environmentally Adjusted NDP and Related Indicators

The most well-known indicator in this category is the eaNDP. Repetto and his colleagues calculated this indicator in their early work on environmental accounting as a way of focusing the attention of policy makers on the importance of environmental degradation and depletion of natural capital. Repetto's work in Indonesia (on petroleum, forests, and land degradation) and Costa Rica (on forests, fisheries, and land degradation) was followed by similar pilot studies in Papua New Guinea and Mexico sponsored by the UN and the World Bank.

Figure 9.2. Percentage Change in Material Use in Five Industrialized Countries, 1975–1996

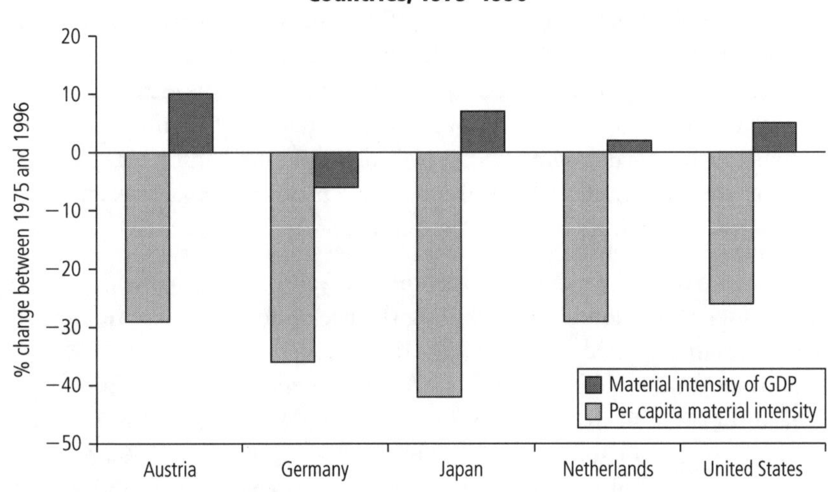

Source: Based on World Resources Institute 2000, table 2, page 20.

Notes: Material intensity calculated as domestic processed output per GDP. Per capita material intensity calculated as domestic processed output per population.

Domestic processed output = domestic extraction + imports − net additions to stock − exports.

More recently, a number of countries have calculated partially adjusted eaNDPs, including Germany, Japan, the Republic of Korea, the Philippines, and Sweden. The great differences among countries in terms of the types of coverage and how the maintenance cost approach was implemented make it impossible to directly compare results across countries. The Republic of Korea, for example, assumed the same abatement costs in all industries, whereas the other countries estimated industry-specific abatement costs.

Sweden's eaNDP, called Genuine Income, shows the least change from conventional NDP, differing only by 0.6 percent. One reason for this very low figure, despite subtracting some environmental protection expenditures, which other countries did not do, is that it measures only environmental degradation from sulfur and nitrogen. Sweden also excluded degradation not already included in conventional measures of NDP, whereas other studies, notably those of the Republic of Korea and the Philippines, did not explicitly address the issue of potential double counting. The adjustment for Japan and Germany are rather large, mainly because they include the estimated cost of reducing carbon emissions (and for Japan, chlorofluorocarbons). The other studies did not address these global pollutants.

Modeling Approaches to Macroeconomic Indicators

Some researchers have criticized eaNDP for combining actual transactions (conventional GDP and NDP) with hypothetical values (monetary value of environmental degradation). The response to this criticism led to the construction of a new set of indicators that seek to estimate what sustainable national income would be if the economy had to change to meet the environmental constraints. Two major approaches were developed—Hueting's SNI and the geNDP.

Hueting's SNI is the maximum income that can be sustained without technological development (excluding the use of nonrenewable resources). Using a static, applied general equilibrium model, SNI has been calculated for the Netherlands in 1990 (Verbruggen and others 2000). The authors found that enormous changes would have to occur in order to fulfill the sustainability standards in the short term: SNI is 56 percent lower than national income in the base year; household consumption declines by 49 percent, government consumption by 69 percent, and net investment by 79 percent.

An alternative approach, the geNDP, estimates national income looking into a hypothetical future in which economic development must meet certain environmental standards. The impact on the economy is estimated by internalizing the costs of reducing environmental degradation. The purpose of this approach is to provide policy makers with guidance about the likely impacts of alternative development paths and the instruments for achieving them. In these models, technology and other model parameters are not always restricted to what is currently available. Estimates for the Netherlands were carried out by De Boer and others (1994). The Swedish National Institute of Economic Research (NIER) (2000) carried out a similar study focusing specifically on carbon dioxide emissions.

General Observations

Much of the use of environmental accounts has been in industrialized countries, especially Australia, Canada, and Europe. The asset accounts are compiled by most countries, but are not generally used to assess sustainability. The flow accounts are widely used, both for the construction of indicators and as inputs to policy modeling. The construction of monetary, environmental macroindicators is quite limited, and it is not clear that these indicators have been much used.

There are, in addition, four main observations regarding how useful environmental accounts are for policy:

- Although some countries are using the environmental accounts quite actively, the accounts are still underutilized, especially in developing countries.
- Very few countries have truly comprehensive environmental accounts.
- International comparisons are important, but not yet possible, because of differences in methodology, coverage, environmental standards, and other factors.
- For a country to fully assess its environmental impact, it must have accounts for the transboundary movement of pollutants via air and water, as well as accounts for its major trading partners to calculate the pollution and material content of products that it imports.

The asset accounts have been used to monitor sustainability in various ways, but many countries have not exploited their full potential to monitor characteristics of wealth and changes in wealth over time. This may be the result of the lack of emphasis on conventional asset accounts and measures of wealth. The lack of a consensus in the revised SEEA about a method for measuring the cost of depletion is also a deterrent. The asset accounts could also be more widely used to assist in resource management. Even simple analysis, such as comparison of rent to the taxes on rent and the costs of resource management, is not routinely carried out in countries that compile asset accounts for natural capital.

The flow accounts are more widely used for the construction of indicators, environmental profiles, and analysis. Considerable overlap occurs between the SEEA and the sustainability indicators proposed by the United Nations, OECD, and other organizations. Tighter links among these different approaches could be useful.

International Comparability

International comparisons are extremely useful for countries in assessing their resource management. The comparisons of water accounts in southern Africa or the environmental damage costs in Europe, for example, are extremely helpful for policy. So far, the comparison of accounts and of the resulting indicators across countries is not generally possible because of the wide range of definitions, coverage, and methodologies used by different countries. Monetary accounts may diverge even more than physical accounts because of the different valuation methodologies, environmental standards, and other assumptions necessary for valuation. With the exception of the genuine saving indicator, it has not been possible to compare monetary environmental macroindicators across countries.

Several studies in Europe have shown that the quantities of pollution exported and imported via air and water are very large. Without accurate information about these quantities, the use of environmental accounts for policy will be limited. Similarly, substantial pollution and resources are embodied in international trade. The Swedish study showed that environmental coefficients (whether of pollution emissions or resource use) can diverge substantially among countries, and that a proper assessment of the environmental impact of a country's imports can only be made with information about the environmental coefficients of one's trading partner, from the partner's environmental accounts. In addition, management of global or regional environmental problems, whether climate change or acidification, require comparable environmental accounts for each country.

Endnote

1. This chapter is mainly drawn from Lange (2003b) and the SEEA, chapter 11.

Appendixes

Sources and Methods

Appendix 1: Building the Wealth Estimates

Appendix 2: Wealth Estimates by Country, 2000

Appendix 3: Genuine Saving Estimates by Country, 2000

Appendix 4: Chanage in Wealth per Capita, 2000

Appendix 1

BUILDING THE WEALTH ESTIMATES

This appendix details the construction of the wealth and genuine saving estimates.

The wealth estimates are composed of the following components:

- Total wealth
- Produced capital
    - Machinery and structures
    - Urban land
- Natural capital
    - Energy resources (oil, natural gas, hard coal, lignite)
    - Mineral resources (bauxite, copper, gold, iron, lead, nickel, phosphate, silver, tin, zinc)
    - Timber resources
    - Nontimber forest resources
    - Cropland
    - Pastureland
    - Protected areas

Intangible capital is calculated as a residual, the difference between total wealth and the sum of produced and natural capital.

Total Wealth

Total wealth can be calculated as $W_t = \int_t^{\infty} C(s) \cdot e^{-r(s-t)} ds$; where W_t is the total value of wealth, or capital, in year t; $C(s)$ is consumption in year s; r is the social rate of return from investment.[1] The social rate of return from investment is equal to: $r = \rho + \eta \frac{\dot{C}}{C}$; where ρ is the pure rate of time preference, η is the elasticity of utility with respect to consumption. Under the assumption that $\eta = 1$, and that consumption grows at a constant rate, then total wealth can be expressed as:

$$W_t = \int_t^{\infty} C(t) \cdot e^{-\rho(s-t)} ds \qquad \text{(A.1)}$$

The current value of total wealth at time t is a function of the consumption at time t and the pure rate of time preference.

Expression (A.1) implicitly assumes that consumption is on a sustainable path, that is, the level of saving is enough to offset the depletion of natural resources. The calculation of total wealth requires that, in computing the initial level of consumption, the following issues be considered:

- *The volatility of consumption.* To solve this problem we used the average of three years of consumption.
- *Negative rates of adjusted net saving.* When adjusted net saving is negative, countries are consuming natural resources, jeopardizing the prospects for future consumption. A measure of sustainable consumption needs to be derived in this instance.

Hence, the following adjustments were made:

- Wealth calculation considered consumption series for 1998–2000.
- For the years in which adjusted net saving was negative, adjusted net saving was subtracted from consumption to obtain *sustainable* consumption, that is, the consumption level that would have left the capital stock intact.
- The corrected consumption series were then expressed in constant 2000 dollars.
- The average of constant dollars consumption between 1998 and 2000 was used as the initial level of consumption.

For computation purposes, we assumed the pure rate of time preference to be 1.5 percent (Pearce and Ulph 1999), and we limited the time horizon to 25 years. This time horizon roughly corresponds to a generation. We adopted the 25-year truncation throughout the calculation of wealth.

Machinery, Equipment, and Structures

For the calculation of physical capital stocks, several estimation procedures can be considered. Some of them, such as the derivation of capital stocks from insurance values or accounting values or from direct surveys, entail enormous expenditures and face problems of limited availability and adequacy of the data. Other estimation procedures, such as the accumulation methods and, in particular, the perpetual inventory method (PIM), are cheaper and more easily implemented since they only require investment data and information on the assets' service life and depreciation patterns. These methods derive capital series from the accumulation of investment series and are the most popular. The PIM is, indeed, the method adopted by most OECD countries that make estimations of capital stocks (Bohm and others 2002; Mas and others 2000; Ward 1976).

In our estimations of capital stocks we also use the PIM. The relevant expression for computing K_t, the aggregate capital stock value in period t, is then given by:

$$K_t = \sum_{i=0}^{19} I_{t-i}(1-\alpha)^i \tag{A.2}$$

where I is the value of investment in constant prices and α is the depreciation rate. In equation (A.2) we implicitly assume that the accumulation period (or service life) is 20 years.[2] The depreciation pattern is geometric with $\alpha = 5$ percent assumed to be constant across countries and over time.[3] Finally, note that equation (A.2) implies a "One-Hoss-Shay" retirement pattern—the value of an asset falls to zero after 20 years.

To estimate equation (A.2) we need long investment series or, alternatively, initial capital stocks.[4] Unfortunately, initial capital stocks are not available for all the countries considered in our estimation, and even in the cases in which there are published data (such as for some OECD, countries), their use would introduce comparability problems with other countries for which those data do not exist.

The investment series for the 65 countries with complete data coverage extend from 1960 to 2000. For 16 countries, complete investment series are not available, but for the missing years we have data on output, final consumption expenditure (private and public), exports, and imports. With this information we can derive investment series from the national accounting identity $Y = C + I + G + (X - M)$ by subtracting net exports from gross domestic saving. In all the cases, the ratios of the investment computed this way and the original investment in the years in which both series are available are very close to one. Still, to ensure the comparability between both investment series, we divided the investment estimates derived from the accounting identity by the country-specific median of these ratios for each country.

With investment series for 81 countries covering the period 1960–2000, it is even possible to compute capital series estimates that go back to 1979. For the rest of the countries for which the original investment series are not complete (because of lack of data on gross-fixed capital formation or on the required terms to apply the national accounting identity over the period 1960–2000), we tried to overcome the data limitations using a quite conservative approach. We extended the investment series by regressing the logarithm of the investment output ratio on time, as in Larson and others (2000). However, we did not extrapolate output, limiting the extension of the investment series to cases in which a corresponding output observation was available.

Urban Land

In the calculation of the value of a country's physical capital stock, the final physical capital estimates include the value of structures, machinery, and equipment, since the value of the stocks is derived (using the perpetual inventory model) from gross capital formation data that account for these elements. In the investment figures, however, only land improvements are captured. Thus, our final capital estimates do not entirely reflect the value of urban land.

Drawing on Kunte and others (1998) urban land was valued as a fixed proportion of the value of physical capital. Ideally, this proportion would be country-specific. In practice, detailed national balance sheet information with which to compute these ratios was not available. Thus, as in Kunte and others (1998), we used a constant proportion equal to 24 percent:[5]

$$U_t = 0.24K_t \qquad \text{(A.3)}$$

Energy and Mineral Resources

In this section, the methodology used in the estimation of the value of nonrenewable resources is described. At least three reasons lie behind the difficulties in such calculations. First, the importance of the inclusion of natural resources in the national accounting systems has been recognized only in the last decades, and although efforts to broaden the national accounts are being made, they are mostly limited to international organizations (such as the UN or the World Bank). Second, there are no private markets for subsoil resource deposits to convey information on the value of these stocks. Third, the stock size is defined in economic terms—reserves are "that part of the reserve base which could be economically extracted or produced at the time of determination"—and, therefore, it is dependent on the prevalent economic conditions, namely technology and prices.[6]

Despite all these difficulties, dollar values were assigned to the stocks of the main energy resources (oil, gas, and coal[7]) and to the stocks of 10 metals and minerals (bauxite, copper, gold, iron ore, lead, nickel, phosphate rock, silver, tin, and zinc) for all the countries that have production figures.

The approach used in our estimation is based on the well-established economic principle that asset values should be measured as the present discounted value of economic profits over the life of the resource. This value, for a particular country and resource, is given by the following expression:

$$V_t = \sum_{i=t}^{t+T-1} \pi_i q_i \Big/ (1+r)^{(i-t)} \tag{A.4}$$

where $\pi_i q_i$ is the economic profit or total rent at time i (π_i denoting unit rent and q_i denoting production), r is the social discount rate, and T is the lifetime of the resource.

Estimating Future Rents

Though well understood and hardly questioned, this approach is rarely used for the practical estimation of natural asset values since it requires the knowledge of actual future rents. Instead, simplifications of (A.4) that implicitly predict future rents based on more or less restrictive assumptions (such as constant total rents, optimality in the extraction path) are used.

The simplification used here assumes that the unit rents grow at rate g: $\frac{\dot{\pi}}{\pi} = g = \frac{r}{1+(\varepsilon-1)(1+r)^T}$, where $\epsilon = 1.15$ is the curvature of the cost function, assumed to be isoelastic (as in Vincent 1996). Then, the effective discount rate is r^*, $r^* = \frac{r-g}{1+g}$, and the value of the resource stock can be expressed as:

$$V_t = \pi_t q_t \left(1+\frac{1}{r^*}\right)\left(1-\frac{1}{(1+r^*)^T}\right) \tag{A.5}$$

This expression is used to value resource stocks when extraction will extend beyond the year 2000.

Choice of T

To guide the choice of an exhaustion-time value, we computed the reserves to production ratios for all the countries, years, and resources.[8] Table A1 provides the median of these ratios for the different resources.

Table A.1 Median Lifetime Years

Energy		Metals and Minerals	
Oil	17	Bauxite	178
Gas	36	Copper	38
Hard coal	122	Gold	16
Soft coal	192	Iron ore	133
		Lead	18
		Nickel	27
		Phosphate	28
		Tin	28
		Silver	22
		Zinc	17

With the exception of the very abundant coal, bauxite, and iron, the reserves-to-production ratios tend to be around 20 to 30 years. As in World Bank (1997), we chose the smaller $T = 20$ for all the resources and countries. From a purely pragmatic point of view, the choice of a longer exhaustion time would demand increasing the time horizon for the predictions of total rents (to feed equation [A.4]). On the other hand, rents obtained further in the future have less weight since they are more heavily discounted. Finally, the level of uncertainty increases the more remote the future is. Under uncertainty, it is unlikely that companies or governments develop reserves to cover more than 20 years worth of production.

Timber Resources

The predominant economic use of forests has been as a source of timber. Timber wealth is calculated as the net present value of rents from roundwood production. The estimation then requires data on roundwood production, unit rents, and the time to exhaustion of the forest (if unsustainably managed).

The annual flow of roundwood production is obtained from the Food and Agriculture Organization of the United Nations database

(FAOSTAT).[9] Calculating the rent is more complex. Theoretically, the value of standing timber is equal to the discounted future stumpage price received by the forest owner after taking out the costs of bringing the timber to maturity. In practice, stumpage prices are usually not readily available, and we calculated unit rents as the product between a composite weighted price times a rental rate.

The composite weighted price of standing timber is estimated as the average of three different prices (weighted by production): (1) the export unit value of coniferous industrial roundwood; (2) export unit value of nonconiferous industrial roundwood; and (3) an estimated world average price of fuelwood. Where country level prices are not available, the regional weighted average is used.[10]

Forestry production-cost data are not available for all countries. Consequently, regional rental rates ([price-cost]/price) were estimated using available studies and consultation with World Bank forestry experts.

Since we applied a market value to standing timber, it was necessary to distinguish between forests available and forests not available for wood supply because some standing timber is simply not accessible or economically viable. The area of forest *available for wood supply* was estimated as forests within 50 kilometers of infrastructure.

Rents were capitalized using a 4 percent discount rate to arrive at a stock of timber resources. The concept of sustainable use of forest resources is introduced via the choice of the time horizon over which the stream is capitalized. If roundwood harvest is smaller than net annual increments, that is, the forest is sustainably harvested, the time horizon is 25 years. If roundwood harvest is greater than the net annual increments, then the time to exhaustion is calculated. The time to exhaustion is based on estimates of forest volume divided by the difference between production and increment. The smaller of 25 years and the time to exhaustion is then used as the resource lifetime.

Roundwood and fuelwood production data are for the year 2000, taken from FAOSTAT forestry data online. Data on industrial roundwood (wood in rough) for coniferous and nonconiferous production were obtained from the United Nations Food and Agriculture Organization (UNFAO 2000) yearbook: *Forest Products 1997–2001*. Fuelwood price data are from FAOSTAT forestry data online. Roundwood export prices are calculated from data from UNFAO *Forestry Products 1997–2001*.

Studies used as a basis for estimating rental rates were Fortech 1997; Whiteman 1996; Tay and others 2001; Lopina and others 2003; Haripriya 1998; Global Witness 2001; Eurostat 2002.

Nontimber Forest Resources

Timber revenues are not the only contribution forests make. Nontimber forest benefits such as minor forest products, hunting, recreation, watershed protection, and option and existence values are significant benefits not usually accounted. This leads to forest resources being undervalued. A review of nontimber forest benefits in developed and developing countries reveals that returns per hectare per year from such benefits vary from $190 per hectare in developed countries to $145 per hectare in developing countries (based on Lampietti and Dixon 1995 and on Croitoru and others 2005, and adjusted to 2000 prices). We assume that only one-tenth of the forest area in each country is accessible, so this per hectare value is multiplied by one-tenth of the forest area in each country to arrive at annual benefits. Nontimber forest resources are then valued as the net present value of benefits over a time horizon of 25 years.[9]

Cropland

Country-level data on agricultural land prices are not widely published, and even if local data were available, it is arguable that land markets are so distorted that a meaningful comparison across countries would be difficult. We have therefore chosen to estimate land values based on the present discounted value of land rents, assuming that the products of the land are sold at world prices.

The return to land is computed as the difference between market value of output crops and crop-specific production costs. Nine representative crops were taken mainly based on their production significance in terms of sowing area, production volume, and revenue. With these three aspects taken into consideration the following nine representative crops were considered: maize, rice, wheat, bananas, grapes, apples, oranges, soybeans, and coffee. Maize, rice, and wheat were calculated individually because they occupy most of the world's agricultural land resources. Bananas, grapes, apples, and oranges were used as proxies for the broader category of fruits and vegetables. Soybeans and coffee were used as proxies for the broader categories of oil crops and beverages, respectively. Roots, pulses, and other crops were calculated as the residual of total arable and permanent cropland minus the sowing areas of the above nine categories.

The annual economic return to land is measured as a percentage of each crop's production revenue, otherwise known as the rental rate. The calculated rental rates were obtained from a series of sector studies. For example, the rental rate for rice uses information on rental rates for the Lao People's Democratic Republic (67.6 percent), Egypt (30.6 percent), and Indonesia (56.1 percent) to obtain a world rental rate for rice of 51 percent. The other rental rates used are 30 percent for maize (from China, Egypt, Yemen), 34 percent for wheat (from Egypt, Yemen, Mongolia, Ecuador), 27 percent for soybeans (from China, Brazil, Argentina), 8 percent for coffee (from Nicaragua, Peru, Vietnam, Costa Rica), 42 percent for bananas (from Brazil, Colombia, Costa Rica, Cote d'Ivoire, Ecuador, Martinique, Suriname, Yemen), 31 percent for grapes (from Moldova, Argentina), 36 percent for apples and oranges (the value is based on the average for bananas and grapes, as no sector studies were found).

The crop-specific ratios are then multiplied by values of production at world prices. This has the effect of assigning higher land rents to more-productive soils. However, applying average crop-specific ratios in this manner probably understates the value of the most-productive lands and overstates the value of the least-productive land within a country.

A country's overall land rent is calculated as a weighted average (weighted by sowing areas) of rents from the 10 crop categories. Return to land for the 10th category (roots, pulses, and other crops) is calculated differently. Since there is no representative crop for it, the land rent is calculated as 80 percent of the weighted average (weighted by sow area) of the three major cereals. This is based on the assumption that roots, pulses, and other crops yield lower returns to land per hectare.

In order to reflect the sustainability of current cultivation practices, the annual return in 2000 is projected to the year 2020 based on growth in production (land areas are assumed to stay constant). Between 2020 and 2024, the value of production was held constant. The growth rates are

0.97 percent and 1.94 percent in developed and developing countries, respectively (Rosengrant and others 1995). The discounted present value of this flow was then calculated using a discount rate of 4 percent.

Pastureland

Pastureland is valued using methods similar to those for cropland. The returns to pastureland are assumed to be a fixed proportion of the value of output. On average, costs of production are 55 percent of revenues, and therefore, returns to pastureland are assumed to be 45 percent of output value. Value of output is based on the production of beef, lamb, milk, and wool valued at international prices. As with croplands, this rental share of output values is applied to country-specific outputs of pastureland valued at world prices. The present value of this flow is then calculated using a 4 percent discount rate over a 25-year time horizon.

In order to reflect the sustainability of current grazing practices, the annual return in 2000 is projected to the year 2020 based on growth in production (land areas are assumed to stay constant). Between 2020 and 2025, the value of production was held constant. The growth rates are 0.89 percent and 2.95 percent in developed and developing countries respectively (Rosengrant and other 1995). The discounted present value of this flow was then calculated using a discount rate of 4 percent.

Protected Areas

Protected areas provide a number of benefits that range from existence values to recreational values. They can be a significant source of income from a thriving tourist industry. These values are revealed by a high willingness to pay for such benefits. The establishment and good maintenance of protected areas preserve an asset for the future, and therefore protected areas form an important part of the natural capital estimates. The willingness to pay to preserve natural regions varies considerably, and there is no comprehensive data set on this.

Protected areas (the World Conservation Union [IUCN] categories I–VI) are valued at the lower of per-hectare returns to pastureland and cropland—a quasi-opportunity cost. These returns are then capitalized over a 25-year time horizon, using a 4 percent discount rate. Limiting the value of protected areas to the opportunity cost of preservation probably captures the minimum value, but not the complete value, of protected areas.

Data on protected areas are taken from the World Database of Protected Areas (WDPA), which is compiled by the United Nations Environment Programme World Conservation Monitoring Centre (UNEP-WCMC). Given the frequent revisions to the database, the data used are for 2003. In the cases of missing data on protected areas, they were assumed to be zero.

Calculating Adjusted Net Saving

Adjusted net saving measures the change in value of a specified set of assets, that is, the investment/disinvestment in different types of capital (produced, human, natural). The calculations are not comprehensive in that they do not include some important sources of environmental degradation such as underground water depletion, unsustainable fisheries, and soil degradation. This results from the lack of internationally comparable data, rather than intended omissions. A detailed description of the methodology to obtain adjusted net saving can be found at the World Bank's Environmental Economics website (www.worldbank.org/environmentaleconomics). The following table summarizes the definitions, data sources, and formulas used in the calculations.

Table A.2 Calculating Adjusted Net Saving

Item	Definition	Formula	Sources	Technical notes	Observations
Gross national saving (GNS)	The difference between GNI and public and private consumption plus net current transfer.	GNS = GNI – private consumption – public consumption + net current transfers	WDI, OECD, UN		
Depreciation (Depr)	The replacement value of capital used up in the process of production.	(data taken directly from source or estimated)	UN	Where country data were unavailable, they were estimated as follows. Available data on depreciation as a percentage of GNI were regressed against the log of GNI per capita. This regression was then used to estimate missing depreciation data. Regression: Dep/GNI = a + (b* Ln(GNI/cap)). The regression was estimated on a five-yearly basis (that is, regression in 1970 was used to estimate depreciation as a percent GNI in years 1970–1974.) Where data were missing for only a couple of years in a country, the same rate of depreciation as a percentage of GNI was applied.	UN data are not available after 1999 for most countries. Missing data are estimated.
Net national saving (NNS)	Difference between gross national saving and the consumption of fixed capital.	NNS = GNS – Depr			
Education expenditure (EE)	Public current operating expenditures in education, including wages and salaries and excluding capital investments in buildings and equipment.	(data taken directly from source or estimated)	Current education expenditure (public): UNESCO	When data are missing, estimation is done as follows: (1) for gaps between two data points, missing information is filled by calculating the average of the two data points; (2) for gaps after the last data point available, missing information is filled on the assumption that education expenditure is a constant share of GNI.	The variable does not include private investment in education. It only includes public expenditures, for which internationally comparable data are available. Notice that education expenditure data are only available up to 1997. One dollar's current expenditure on education does not necessarily yield exactly one dollar's worth of human capital (see, for example, Jorgensen and Fraumeni 1992). However, an adjustment from standard national accounts is needed. In national accounts, nonfixed-capital expenditures on education are treated strictly as consumption. If a country's human capital is to be regarded as a valuable asset, expenditures on its formation must be seen as an investment.

Item	Definition	Formula	Sources	Technical notes	Observations
Energy depletion (ED)	Product of unit resource rents and the physical quantities of energy extracted. It covers coal, crude oil, and natural gas.	ED = production volume * average international market price * unit resource rent	Quantities: OECD, British Petroleum, International Energy Agency, International Petroleum Encyclopedia, United Nations, World Bank, national sources. Prices: OECD, British Petroleum, national sources. Costs: IEA, World Bank, national sources	Energy depletion covers crude oil, natural gas, and coal (hard and lignite). Unit resource rent is calculated as (unit world price – average cost) / unit world price. Notice that marginal cost should be used instead of average cost in order to calculate the true opportunity cost of extraction. Marginal cost is, however, difficult to compute.	Prices refer to international rather than local prices, to reflect the social cost of energy depletion. This differs from national accounts methodologies, which may use local prices to measure energy GDP. This difference explains eventual discrepancies in the values for energy depletion and energy GDP.
Mineral depletion (MD)	Product of unit resource rents and the physical quantities of mineral extracted. It covers tin, gold, lead, zinc, iron, copper, nickel, silver, bauxite, and phosphate.	MD = production volume * average international market price * unit resource rent	Quantitites: USGS (2005) mineral yearbook. Prices: UNCTAD monthly commodity price bulletin. Costs: World Bank, national sources	Mineral depletion covers tin, gold, lead, zinc, iron, copper, nickel, silver, bauxite, and phosphate. Unit resource rent is calculated as (unit price – average cost) / unit price. Notice that marginal cost should be used instead of average cost in order to calculate the true opportunity cost of extraction. Marginal cost is, however, difficult to compute.	Prices refer to international rather than local prices, to reflect the social cost of energy depletion. This differs from national accounts methodologies, which may use local prices to measure mineral GDP. This difference explains eventual discrepancies in the values for mineral depletion and mineral GDP.
Net forest depletion (NFD)	Product of unit resource rents and the excess of roundwood harvest over natural growth.	NFD = (roundwood production –increment) * average price * rental rate	Round wood production: FAOSTAT forestry database. Increments: World Bank, FAO, UNECE, WRI, country-specific sources. Rental rates: various sources	In a country where increment exceeded wood extraction, no adjustment to net adjusted saving was made, no matter what the absolute volume or value of wood extracted. Increment per hectare on productive forest land is adjusted to allow for country-specific characteristics of the timber industry.	Net forest depletion is not the monetary value of deforestation. Data on roundwood and fuelwood production are different from deforestation, which represents a permanent change in land use, and thus is not comparable. Areas logged out but intended for regeneration are not included in deforestation figures (see WDI definition of deforestation), but are counted as producing timber depletion. Net forest depletion only includes timber values and does not include the loss of nontimber forest benefits and nonuse benefits.
CO_2 damages (CO_2D)	A conservative figure of $20 marginal global damages per ton of carbon emitted was taken from Fankhauser (1994).	CO_2D = emissions (tons) * $20	Data on carbon emissions can be obtained from the WDI	Data lag by several years so the data for missing years are estimated. This is done by taking the ratio of average emissions from the last three years of available data to the average of the last three years' GDP in constant local currency unit. This ratio is then applied to the missing years' GDP to estimate carbon dioxide emissions. The atomic weight of carbon is 12 and for carbon dioxide 44, and carbon is only (12/44) of the emissions. Damages are estimated per ton but the emissions data are per kilo ton. The CO_2 emissions data have therefore been multiplied by 20*(12/44)*1000.	CO_2 damages include the social cost of permanent damages caused by CO_2 emissions. This may differ (sometimes in large measure) from the *market* value of CO_2 emissions reductions traded in emissions markets.

Item	Definition	Formula	Sources	Technical notes	Observations
PM_{10} damages ($PM_{10}D$)	Willingness to pay to avoid mortality and morbidity attributable to particulate emissions.	$PM_{10}D$ = disability adjusted life years lost due to PM emissions * WTP			
Adjusted net saving (ANS)	Net national saving plus education expenditure and minus energy depletion, mineral depletion, net forest depletion, carbon dioxide damage, and particulate emissions damage.	$ANS = NNS + EE - ED - MD - NFD - CO_2D - PM_{10}D$			

Source: Authors.

Endnotes

1. A proof that the current value of wealth is equal to the net present value of consumption can be found in Hamilton and Hartwick 2005.

2. The choice of a service life of 20 years tries to reflect the mix of relatively long-lived structures and short-lived machinery and equipment in the aggregate capital stock and investment series. In a study that derives cross-country capital estimates for 62 countries, Larson and others (2000) also use a mean service life of 20 years for aggregate investment.

3. Again, by choosing a 5 percent depreciation rate we try to capture the diversity of assets included in the aggregate investment series.

4. That is, $K_t = \sum_{i=0}^{t} I_{t-i}(1-\alpha)^i + K_0$ for $t < 20$.

5. Kunte and others (1998) based their estimation of urban land value on Canada's detailed national balance sheet information. Urban land is estimated to be 33 percent of the value of structures, which in turn is estimated to be 72 percent of the total value of physical capital.

6. U.S. Geological Survey definition. It is clear that an increase in, say, oil price or a reduction in its extraction costs would increase the amount of "economically extractable" oil and therefore increase the reserves. Indeed, U.S. oil production has surpassed several times the proved reserves in 1950.

7. Coal is subdivided into two groups: hard coal (anthracite and bituminous) and soft coal (lignite and subbituminous).

8. The World Bank database provides good coverage on production data for the 14 resources. Oil and gas reserves data from various issues of *The Gas and Oil Journal* are also fairly complete. However, reserves data on coal from *The World Energy Conference* and on metals and minerals from the U.S. Bureau of Mines' *Mineral Commodity Summaries* are less complete. In fact, for the 10 metals and minerals, the reserves-to-production ratios were computed for a limited number of countries starting in 1987, due to data limitations.

9. When data are missing and if a country's forest area is less than 50 square kilometers, the value of production is assumed to be zero.

10. After consultation with World Bank forestry experts, some country-level prices were replaced by the regional average.

Appendix 2

Wealth Estimates by Country, 2000

Wealth Estimates by Country, 2000, $ per Capita

Country name	Population	Subsoil assets	Timber resources	NTFR	PA	Cropland	Pastureland	Natural capital	Produced capital + urban land	Intangible capital	Total wealth
Albania	3,113,000	300	38	72	247	1,660	1,574	3,892	1,745	11,675	17,312
Algeria	30,385,000	11,670	68	16	161	859	426	13,200	8,709	−3,418	18,491
Antigua and Barbuda	72,310	0	0	28	0	1,003	468	1,500	38,796	91,554	131,849
Argentina	35,850,000	3,253	105	219	350	3,632	2,754	10,312	19,111	109,809	139,232
Australia	19,182,000	11,491	748	551	1,421	4,365	5,590	24,167	58,179	288,686	371,031
Austria	8,012,000	485	829	144	2,410	1,298	2,008	7,174	73,118	412,789	493,080
Bangladesh	131,050,000	83	4	2	9	810	52	961	817	4,221	6,000
Barbados	267,000	988	0	0	0	190	210	1,388	18,168	127,181	146,737
Belgium-Luxembourg	10,690,000	20	254	20	0	575	2,161	3,030	60,561	388,123	451,714
Belize	240,000	0	344	1,272	0	5,201	133	6,950	9,710	36,275	52,935
Benin	6,222,000	15	321	96	207	603	90	1,333	771	5,791	7,895
Bhutan	805,000	0	1,888	849	1,291	589	328	4,945	2,622	180	7,747
Bolivia	8,428,000	934	100	1,426	232	1,550	541	4,783	2,110	11,248	18,141
Botswana	1,675,000	246	172	1,681	299	55	730	3,183	8,926	28,483	40,592
Brazil	170,100,000	1,708	609	724	402	1,998	1,311	6,752	9,643	70,528	86,922
Bulgaria	8,170,000	244	126	102	217	1,650	1,108	3,448	5,303	16,505	25,256
Burkina Faso	11,274,000	0	239	142	100	547	191	1,219	821	3,047	5,087
Burundi	6,807,000	4	23	3	7	1,130	44	1,210	206	1,443	2,859
Cameroon	15,117,000	914	348	357	187	2,748	179	4,733	1,749	4,271	10,753
Canada	30,770,000	18,566	4,724	1,264	5,756	2,829	1,631	34,771	54,226	235,982	324,979
Cape Verde	435,000	0	0	44	0	585	82	711	3,902	28,329	32,942

Country name	Population	Subsoil assets	Timber resources	NTFR	PA	Cropland	Pastureland	Natural capital	Produced capital + urban land	Intangible capital	Total wealth
Chad	7,861,000	0	311	366	80	787	316	1,861	289	2,307	4,458
Chile	15,211,000	5,188	986	231	1,095	2,443	1,001	10,944	10,688	56,094	77,726
China	1,262,644,992	511	106	29	27	1,404	146	2,223	2,956	4,208	9,387
Colombia	42,299,000	3,006	134	266	253	1,911	978	6,547	4,872	33,241	44,660
Comoros	558,000	0	17	3	0	872	75	967	1,270	5,792	8,030
Congo, Rep. of	3,447,000	7,536	0	1,450	3	329	13	9,330	6,343	–12,158	3,516
Costa Rica	3,810,000	2	629	117	657	5,811	1,310	8,527	8,343	44,741	61,611
Côte d'Ivoire	15,827,000	2	367	102	11	2,568	72	3,121	997	10,125	14,243
Denmark	5,340,000	4,173	211	25	1,377	2,184	3,775	11,746	80,181	483,212	575,138
Dominica	71,530	0	..	146	0	5,274	553	5,973	15,310	37,802	59,084
Dominican Republic	8,353,000	286	27	37	461	1,980	386	3,176	5,723	24,511	33,410
Ecuador	12,420,000	5,205	335	193	1,057	5,263	1,065	13,117	2,841	17,788	33,745
Egypt, Arab Rep. of	63,976,000	1,544	0	0	0	1,705	0	3,249	3,897	14,734	21,879
El Salvador	6,209,000	0	105	4	4	404	395	912	4,109	31,455	36,476
Estonia	1,370,000	384	1,382	341	490	1,114	2,572	6,283	18,685	41,802	66,769
Ethiopia	64,298,000	0	63	16	167	353	197	796	177	992	1,965
Fiji	812,000	77	0	227	0	1,381	522	2,208	4,192	38,480	44,880
Finland	5,172,000	58	6,115	1,259	1,090	843	2,081	11,445	61,064	346,838	419,346
France	58,893,000	87	307	77	1,026	2,747	2,091	6,335	57,814	403,874	468,024
Gabon	1,258,000	24,656	1,570	841	1	1,480	37	28,586	17,797	–3,215	43,168
Gambia, The	1,312,000	0	0	83	4	345	81	514	672	5,179	6,365
Georgia	5,262,000	66	0	129	66	737	802	1,799	595	10,642	13,036
Germany	82,210,000	269	263	39	1,113	1,176	1,586	4,445	68,678	423,323	496,447
Ghana	18,912,080	65	290	76	7	855	43	1,336	686	8,343	10,365
Greece	10,560,000	318	82	101	57	3,424	573	4,554	28,973	203,445	236,972
Grenada	101,400	0	0	0	0	572	67	640	16,128	38,544	55,312
Guatemala	11,385,000	301	517	57	181	1,697	218	2,971	3,098	24,411	30,480
Guinea-Bissau	1,367,000	0	195	362	0	1,180	121	1,858	549	1,566	3,974
Guyana	759,000	1,147	680	2,886	12	5,324	252	10,301	3,333	2,176	15,810
Haiti	7,959,000	0	8	3	3	668	112	793	601	6,840	8,235
Honduras	6,457,000	24	727	189	282	1,189	595	3,005	3,064	5,497	11,567
Hungary	10,024,000	536	152	42	366	2,721	1,131	4,947	15,480	56,645	77,072

Country name	Population	Subsoil assets	Timber resources	NTFR	PA	Cropland	Pastureland	Natural capital	Produced capital + urban land	Intangible capital	Total wealth
India	1,015,923,008	201	59	14	122	1,340	192	1,928	1,154	3,738	6,820
Indonesia	206,264,992	1,549	346	115	167	1,245	50	3,472	2,382	8,015	13,869
Iran, Islamic Rep. of	63,664,000	11,370	0	26	109	1,989	611	14,105	3,336	6,581	24,023
Ireland	3,813,000	385	222	51	172	1,583	8,122	10,534	46,542	273,414	330,490
Israel	6,289,000	10	0	6	1,350	1,757	877	3,999	44,153	246,570	294,723
Italy	57,690,000	361	0	51	543	2,639	1,083	4,678	51,943	316,045	372,666
Jamaica	2,580,000	856	157	29	609	824	152	2,627	10,153	35,016	47,796
Japan	126,870,000	28	38	56	364	710	316	1,513	150,258	341,470	493,241
Jordan	4,887,000	9	16	4	89	580	234	931	5,875	24,740	31,546
Kenya	30,092,000	1	235	129	113	361	529	1,368	868	4,374	6,609
Korea, Rep. of	47,008,000	33	0	30	441	1,241	275	2,020	31,399	107,864	141,282
Latvia	2,372,000	0	1,155	279	668	1,506	1,877	5,485	12,979	28,734	47,198
Lesotho	1,744,000	0	4	2	1	239	269	515	3,263	11,699	15,477
Madagascar	15,523,000	0	174	171	36	955	345	1,681	395	2,944	5,020
Malawi	10,311,000	0	184	56	26	474	45	785	542	3,873	5,200
Malaysia	23,270,000	6,922	438	188	161	1,369	24	9,103	13,065	24,520	46,687
Mali	10,840,000	0	121	276	44	1,420	295	2,157	621	2,463	5,241
Mauritania	2,508,159	1,311	14	29	21	1,128	480	2,982	1,038	3,938	7,959
Mauritius	1,187,000	0	0	3	0	577	62	642	11,633	48,010	60,284
Mexico	97,966,000	6,075	199	128	176	1,195	721	8,493	18,959	34,420	61,872
Moldova	4,278,000	0	3	17	52	2,435	752	3,260	4,338	1,173	8,771
Morocco	28,705,000	106	22	24	7	993	453	1,604	3,435	17,926	22,965
Mozambique	17,691,000	0	340	392	9	261	57	1,059	478	2,695	4,232
Namibia	1,894,000	46	0	962	260	204	881	2,352	5,574	28,981	36,907
Nepal	23,043,000	0	233	38	81	767	111	1,229	609	1,964	3,802
Netherlands	15,919,000	2,053	27	7	527	1,035	3,090	6,739	62,428	352,222	421,389
New Zealand	3,858,000	3,596	1,648	611	11,786	5,824	19,761	43,226	36,227	163,481	242,934
Nicaragua	5,071,000	9	475	146	184	867	410	2,092	1,719	9,403	13,214
Niger	10,742,000	1	9	28	152	1,598	187	1,975	286	1,434	3,695
Nigeria	126,910,000	2,639	270	24	6	1,022	78	4,040	667	−1,959	2,748
Norway	4,491,000	49,839	573	586	1,339	567	1,925	54,828	119,650	299,230	473,708
Pakistan	138,080,000	265	7	4	94	549	448	1,368	975	5,529	7,871
Panama	2,854,000	0	176	228	726	3,256	664	5,051	11,018	41,594	57,663
Paraguay	5,270,000	0	882	1,005	78	2,193	1,215	5,372	4,480	25,747	35,600
Peru	25,939,000	934	153	570	98	1,480	341	3,575	5,562	29,908	39,046

Country name	Population	Subsoil assets	Timber resources	NTFR	PA	Cropland	Pastureland	Natural capital	Produced capital + urban land	Intangible capital	Total wealth
Philippines	76,627,000	30	90	17	59	1,308	45	1,549	2,673	15,129	19,351
Portugal	10,130,000	41	438	107	385	1,724	934	3,629	31,011	172,837	207,477
Romania	22,435,000	1,222	290	65	175	1,602	1,154	4,508	8,495	16,110	29,113
Russian Federation	145,555,008	11,777	292	1,228	1,317	1,262	1,342	17,217	15,593	5,900	38,709
Rwanda	7,709,000	2	81	9	27	1,849	98	2,066	549	3,055	5,670
Senegal	9,530,000	4	238	147	78	608	196	1,272	975	7,920	10,167
Seychelles	81,131	0	0	84	0	0	0	84	28,836	96,653	125,572
Singapore	4,018,000	0	0	0	0	0	0	0	79,011	173,595	252,607
South Africa	44,000,000	1,118	310	46	51	1,238	637	3,400	7,270	48,959	59,629
Spain	40,500,000	50	81	105	360	2,806	971	4,374	39,531	217,300	261,205
Sri Lanka	18,467,000	0	58	24	166	485	84	817	2,710	11,204	14,731
St. Kitts and Nevis	44,286	0	0	0	0	0	0	0	35,711	64,457	100,167
St. Lucia	155,996	0	0	13	0	3,394	108	3,516	13,594	49,090	66,199
St. Vincent	111,992	0	0	12	0	2,106	109	2,228	10,486	36,518	49,232
Suriname	425,000	4,451	293	1,173	7,626	2,113	210	15,866	5,818	25,444	47,128
Swaziland	1,045,000	0	314	113	0	372	467	1,267	3,628	22,844	27,739
Sweden	8,869,000	263	2,434	908	1,549	1,120	1,676	7,950	58,331	447,143	513,424
Switzerland	7,180,000	0	493	50	2,195	809	2,396	5,943	99,904	542,394	648,241
Syrian Arab Rep.	16,189,000	6,734	0	6	0	1,255	730	8,725	3,292	−1,598	10,419
Thailand	60,728,000	469	92	55	855	2,370	96	3,936	7,624	24,294	35,854
Togo	4,562,000	7	163	25	21	649	50	915	800	5,394	7,109
Trinidad and Tobago	1,289,000	30,279	42	46	112	444	54	30,977	14,485	12,086	57,549
Tunisia	9,564,000	1,610	27	12	8	1,546	736	3,939	6,270	26,328	36,537
Turkey	67,420,000	190	64	34	86	2,270	861	3,504	8,580	35,774	47,859
United Kingdom	58,880,000	4,739	44	14	495	583	1,291	7,167	55,239	346,347	408,753
United States	282,224,000	7,106	1,341	238	1,651	2,752	1,665	14,752	79,851	418,009	512,612
Uruguay	3,322,000	0	0	88	22	3,621	5,549	9,279	10,787	98,397	118,463
Venezuela, R. B. de	24,170,000	23,302	0	464	1,793	1,086	581	27,227	13,627	4,342	45,196
Zambia	9,886,000	134	276	716	78	477	98	1,779	694	4,091	6,564
Zimbabwe	12,650,000	301	211	341	70	350	258	1,531	1,377	6,704	9,612

Source: Authors.
Note: NTFR: non-timber forest resources; PA: protected areas.

Appendix 3

Genuine Saving Estimates by Country, 2000

Revenue Saving, 2000, % of GNI

Country name	Gross national saving	Consumption of fixed capital	Net national saving	Education expenditure	Energy depletion	Mineral depletion	Net forest depletion	PM_{10} damage*	CO_2 damage	Genuine saving
Afghanistan	..	..	..	..	..	..	..	..	..	..
Albania	19.4	9.0	10.4	2.8	1.4	0.0	0.0	0.1	0.4	11.4
Algeria	41.1	11.2	29.9	4.5	39.7	0.1	0.1	0.7	1.0	–7.3
American Samoa	..	..	..	..	..	..	..	..	..	..
Andorra	..	..	..	..	..	..	..	..	..	..
Angola	54.8	10.6	44.2	4.4	55.9	0.0	0.0	..	0.5	..
Antigua and Barbuda	19.4	12.6	6.8	3.7	0.0	0.0	0.0	..	0.3	..
Argentina	13.4	12.1	1.3	3.2	2.4	0.1	0.0	1.6	0.3	0.1
Armenia	4.0	8.1	–4.2	1.8	0.0	0.1	0.0	2.0	1.1	–5.4
Aruba	..	..	..	..	..	..	..	..	..	..
Australia	19.5	16.1	3.4	4.9	1.8	1.5	0.0	0.1	0.5	4.3
Austria	22.0	14.5	7.5	5.6	0.1	0.0	0.0	0.2	0.2	12.5
Azerbaijan	18.1	14.9	3.2	3.0	54.5	0.0	0.0	1.0	3.5	–52.7
Bahamas, The	..	13.2	..	3.8	0.0	0.0	0.0	..	0.2	..
Bahrain	27.1	12.7	14.4	4.4	17.6	0.0	0.0	..	1.5	..
Bangladesh	25.8	5.9	19.9	1.3	1.3	0.0	0.8	0.3	0.4	18.5
Barbados	12.1	12.4	–0.4	7.2	0.6	0.0	0.0	..	0.3	..
Belarus	23.8	9.2	14.5	5.4	2.9	0.0	0.0	0.0	2.7	14.3
Belgium	24.3	14.4	9.9	3.0	0.0	0.0	0.0	0.2	0.3	12.5
Belize	9.2	6.0	3.2	6.2	0.0	0.0	0.0	..	0.6	..
Benin	10.4	7.7	2.7	2.7	0.2	0.0	1.4	0.3	0.4	3.1
Bermuda	..	..	..	3.3	..	..	..	..	..	..
Bhutan	32.9	9.3	23.6	2.4	0.0	0.0	5.2	..	0.5	..
Bolivia	11.1	9.2	1.8	4.8	4.8	0.8	0.0	0.7	0.8	–0.6
Bosnia and Herzegovina	20.8	8.7	12.0	..	0.2	0.0	0.0	0.4	2.4	..

Country name	Gross national saving	Consumption of fixed capital	Net national saving	Education expenditure	Energy depletion	Mineral depletion	Net forest depletion	PM_{10} damage*	CO_2 damage	Genuine saving
Botswana	41.9	12.1	29.8	5.6	0.0	0.5	0.0	..	0.5	..
Brazil	17.8	11.0	6.8	3.7	2.0	0.8	0.0	0.2	0.3	7.2
Brunei	..	..	..	2.9	..	..	..	..	..	..
Bulgaria	13.0	9.8	3.2	3.0	0.3	0.6	0.0	2.1	2.0	1.1
Burkina Faso	11.0	7.1	4.0	2.4	0.0	0.0	0.0	0.5	0.2	5.6
Burundi	0.9	6.1	–5.2	4.0	0.0	0.0	8.7	0.1	0.2	–10.2
Cambodia	14.1	7.6	6.5	1.4	0.0	0.0	1.2	0.1	0.1	6.6
Cameroon	14.6	8.9	5.7	2.3	9.4	0.0	0.0	0.7	0.5	–2.5
Canada	24.6	13.1	11.5	6.9	4.9	0.2	0.0	0.2	0.4	12.7
Cape Verde	9.2	9.5	–0.3	3.9	0.0	0.0	0.0	..	0.2	..
Cayman Islands	..	..	..	..	..	..	..	..	..	..
Central African Republic	6.7	7.3	–0.6	1.6	0.0	0.0	0.0	0.4	0.2	0.5
Chad	0.7	6.8	–6.1	1.4	0.0	0.0	0.0	..	0.1	..
Channel Islands	..	..	..	..	..	..	..	..	..	..
Chile	21.3	10.0	11.3	3.5	0.3	6.0	0.0	1.0	0.5	7.0
China	38.8	8.9	29.8	2.0	3.6	0.3	0.1	1.0	1.6	25.5
Colombia	15.5	10.2	5.3	3.1	8.4	0.3	0.0	0.1	0.4	–0.9
Comoros	–1.2	7.6	–8.9	4.2	0.0	0.0	0.0	..	0.2	..
Congo, Dem. Rep. of	–4.6	6.9	–11.5	0.9	3.3	0.3	0.0	0.0	0.4	–14.6
Congo, Rep. of	41.0	12.6	28.4	5.9	68.2	0.5	0.0	..	0.5	..
Costa Rica	13.6	6.2	7.4	5.0	0.0	0.0	0.4	0.3	0.2	11.5
Côte d'Ivoire	8.4	9.1	–0.7	4.5	4.1	0.0	0.6	0.6	0.6	–2.1
Croatia	18.1	11.1	7.0	..	1.3	0.0	0.0	0.3	0.6	..
Cuba	..	..	..	6.1	..	..	..	..	..	..
Cyprus	..	10.6	..	5.3	0.0	0.0	0.0	..	0.4	..
Czech Republic	24.5	11.5	13.0	3.9	0.1	0.0	0.0	0.1	1.3	15.4
Denmark	23.5	15.4	8.1	7.9	0.9	0.0	0.0	0.1	0.2	14.8
Djibouti	–2.4	8.5	–10.9	..	0.0	0.0	0.0	..	0.4	..
Dominica	5.7	12.2	–6.6	5.0	0.0	0.0	0.0	..	0.3	..
Dominican Republic	19.2	5.4	13.8	2.0	0.0	0.6	0.0	0.2	0.8	14.2
Ecuador	28.3	10.2	18.1	3.2	25.6	0.0	0.0	0.1	1.0	–5.5
Egypt, Arab Rep. of	16.7	9.5	7.2	4.4	5.6	0.1	0.2	1.4	0.8	3.6
El Salvador	13.9	10.2	3.7	2.4	0.0	0.0	0.7	0.2	0.3	5.0
Equatorial Guinea	..	31.2	..	..	0.0	0.0	0.0	..	0.3	..
Eritrea	28.1	5.3	22.8	1.4	0.0	0.0	0.0	0.5	0.5	23.2
Estonia	23.2	14.2	9.0	6.3	0.5	0.0	0.0	0.2	1.8	12.8
Ethiopia	10.5	6.0	4.5	4.0	0.0	0.1	12.4	0.3	0.5	–4.8

Country name	Gross national saving	Consumption of fixed capital	Net national saving	Education expenditure	Energy depletion	Mineral depletion	Net forest depletion	PM_{10} damage*	CO_2 damage	Genuine saving
Faeroe Islands	..	..	..	..	..	..	..	..	..	..
Fiji	4.9	10.4	–5.4	4.6	0.0	0.2	0.0	..	0.3	..
Finland	28.3	16.4	12.0	7.0	0.0	0.0	0.0	0.1	0.3	18.6
France	22.0	12.6	9.4	5.1	0.0	0.0	0.0	0.0	0.2	14.3
French Polynesia	..	12.6	..	..	0.0	0.0	0.0	..	0.1	..
Gabon	16.6	12.6	4.0	2.7	41.8	0.0	0.0	0.1	0.5	–35.7
Gambia, The	3.4	7.9	–4.4	3.4	0.0	0.0	0.5	0.7	0.4	–2.6
Georgia	12.7	15.6	–2.9	4.3	0.8	0.0	0.0	2.5	1.2	–3.0
Germany	20.3	14.9	5.4	4.3	0.1	0.0	0.0	0.1	0.2	9.3
Ghana	15.6	7.3	8.4	2.8	0.0	1.5	3.3	0.2	0.7	5.6
Greece	19.1	8.7	10.4	3.1	0.1	0.1	0.0	0.7	0.5	12.2
Greenland	..	..	..	..	..	..	..	..	..	..
Grenada	24.1	11.9	12.3	5.4	0.0	0.0	0.0	..	0.3	..
Guam	..	..	..	..	..	..	..	..	..	..
Guatemala	12.6	9.8	2.8	1.6	1.1	0.0	1.1	0.2	0.3	1.7
Guinea	17.2	8.0	9.1	2.0	0.0	3.7	1.9	0.6	0.3	4.8
Guinea-Bissau	–15.1	6.9	–22.1	..	0.0	0.0	0.0	..	0.8	..
Guyana	7.9	9.6	–1.7	3.3	0.0	7.2	0.0	..	1.4	..
Haiti	27.7	1.8	25.9	1.5	0.0	0.0	0.8	0.2	0.2	26.1
Honduras	25.9	5.6	20.3	3.5	0.0	0.1	0.0	0.2	0.5	23.0
Hong Kong, China	31.8	13.1	18.7	2.8	0.0	0.0	0.0	0.0	0.1	21.4
Hungary	23.1	11.8	11.3	4.9	0.7	0.0	0.0	0.4	0.7	14.4
Iceland	14.8	13.5	1.2	5.2	0.0	0.0	0.0	..	0.2	..
India	24.2	9.6	14.6	3.9	2.3	0.4	0.9	0.7	1.4	12.9
Indonesia	21.0	5.6	15.4	1.4	12.5	1.4	0.0	0.5	1.1	1.3
Iran, Islamic Rep. of	38.0	9.1	28.8	4.0	41.7	0.2	0.0	0.7	1.8	–11.5
Iraq	..	..	..	..	..	..	..	..	..	..
Ireland	29.5	11.9	17.6	5.7	0.0	0.1	0.0	0.1	0.3	22.7
Isle of Man	..	..	..	..	..	..	..	..	..	..
Israel	17.2	15.1	2.1	6.8	0.0	0.1	0.0	0.0	0.3	8.5
Italy	20.1	13.7	6.5	4.4	0.1	0.0	0.0	0.2	0.2	10.3
Jamaica	22.5	11.0	11.6	5.9	0.0	1.5	0.0	0.3	0.8	14.8
Japan	28.4	15.9	12.5	3.1	0.0	0.0	0.0	0.4	0.1	15.1
Jordan	21.0	10.6	10.4	5.0	0.3	1.3	0.0	0.7	1.1	11.9
Kazakhstan	23.3	9.9	13.4	4.4	41.5	1.0	0.0	0.4	4.2	–29.2
Kenya	13.4	7.7	5.7	6.0	0.0	0.0	0.1	0.2	0.5	10.9
Kiribati	..	4.8	..	..	0.0	0.0	0.0	..	0.2	..
Korea, Dem. People's Republic of	..	..	..	..	..	..	..	..	..	..

Country name	Gross national saving	Consumption of fixed capital	Net national saving	Education expenditure	Energy depletion	Mineral depletion	Net forest depletion	PM_{10} damage*	CO_2 damage	Genuine saving
Korea, Rep. of	34.0	12.2	21.7	3.1	0.0	0.0	0.0	0.8	0.5	23.6
Kuwait	40.0	6.5	33.5	5.0	48.7	0.0	0.0	2.0	0.6	–12.9
Kyrgyz Republic	15.5	7.8	7.7	3.4	1.3	0.0	0.0	0.2	2.1	7.4
Lao PDR	21.1	7.7	13.4	1.8	0.0	0.0	0.0	0.2	0.1	14.8
Latvia	18.2	10.7	7.5	5.1	0.0	0.0	0.0	0.3	0.5	11.8
Lebanon	2.1	10.2	–8.1	2.5	0.0	0.0	0.0	0.6	0.5	–6.6
Lesotho	16.9	6.4	10.5	7.3	0.0	0.0	2.1	0.4	..	..
Liberia	..	8.5	..	..	0.0	8.0	2.3	0.0	0.6	..
Libya	..	..	..	..	..	..	..	..	..	..
Liechtenstein	..	..	..	..	..	..	..	..	..	..
Lithuania	13.9	10.2	3.7	5.2	0.5	0.0	0.0	0.7	0.6	7.1
Luxembourg	36.0	13.4	22.6	3.7	0.0	0.0	0.0	..	0.3	..
Macao, China	47.2	12.6	34.6	3.6	0.0	0.0	0.0	..	0.2	..
Macedonia, FYR	23.5	9.9	13.6	4.9	0.0	0.0	0.0	0.3	1.9	16.3
Madagascar	9.0	7.3	1.7	1.8	0.0	0.0	0.0	0.2	0.4	2.9
Malawi	3.0	6.8	–3.8	4.4	0.0	0.0	1.6	0.2	0.3	–1.4
Malaysia	40.1	11.8	28.3	4.7	11.4	0.0	0.0	0.1	1.0	20.5
Maldives	36.8	10.6	26.2	6.1	0.0	0.0	0.0	..	0.5	..
Mali	13.9	7.1	6.8	2.1	0.0	0.0	0.0	0.5	0.1	8.3
Malta	15.4	7.5	7.9	4.9	0.0	0.0	0.0	..	0.4	..
Marshall Islands	..	7.8	..	..	0.0	0.0	0.0	..	..	..
Mauritania	16.7	7.5	9.1	3.7	0.0	19.9	0.8	..	1.9	..
Mauritius	25.1	10.8	14.2	3.3	0.0	0.0	0.0	..	0.4	..
Mayotte	..	..	..	..	..	..	..	..	..	..
Mexico	21.0	10.6	10.4	5.0	5.9	0.1	0.0	0.5	0.4	8.4
Micronesia, Federated States of	..	8.9	..	..	0.0	0.0	0.0	..	..	..
Moldova	15.6	7.1	8.6	3.5	0.0	0.0	0.0	0.5	2.9	8.7
Monaco	..	..	..	..	..	..	..	..	..	..
Mongolia	29.1	10.8	18.3	5.7	0.0	1.9	0.0	0.5	4.7	16.8
Morocco	22.9	9.4	13.4	4.8	0.0	0.6	0.0	0.2	0.7	16.8
Mozambique	11.2	7.4	3.8	3.8	0.0	0.0	0.0	0.4	0.2	7.0
Myanmar	..	..	..	0.9	..	..	..	..	..	..
N. Mariana Islands	..	..	..	..	..	..	..	..	..	..
Namibia	27.5	13.1	14.4	7.4	0.0	0.3	0.0	0.2	0.3	21.0
Nepal	21.8	2.4	19.5	3.2	0.0	0.0	3.3	0.1	0.4	18.9
Netherlands	26.1	14.7	11.4	4.9	0.5	0.0	0.0	0.4	0.2	15.1
Netherlands Antilles	..	..	..	..	..	..	..	..	..	..

Country name	Gross national saving	Consumption of fixed capital	Net national saving	Education expenditure	Energy depletion	Mineral depletion	Net forest depletion	PM_{10} damage*	CO_2 damage	Genuine saving
New Caledonia	..	12.4	..	..	0.0	0.0	0.0	..	0.4	..
New Zealand	17.7	10.9	6.8	6.9	1.3	0.1	0.0	0.0	0.4	11.8
Nicaragua	17.3	9.1	8.2	3.7	0.0	0.1	0.9	0.0	0.6	10.3
Niger	2.6	6.7	–4.0	2.3	0.0	0.0	4.1	0.4	0.4	–6.7
Nigeria	25.7	8.4	17.3	0.9	50.8	0.0	0.0	0.8	0.6	–33.9
Norway	36.9	16.2	20.7	6.1	8.0	0.0	0.0	0.1	0.2	18.5
Oman	29.9	11.7	18.1	3.9	47.8	0.0	0.0	..	0.6	..
Pakistan	19.9	7.8	12.1	2.3	3.1	0.0	0.8	1.0	0.9	8.6
Palau	..	10.9	..	..	0.0	0.0	0.0	..	1.2	..
Panama	24.9	7.9	17.0	4.5	0.0	0.0	0.0	0.3	0.3	20.8
Papua New Guinea	..	8.9	..	..	17.8	11.7	0.0	0.0	0.4	..
Paraguay	14.5	9.5	5.0	3.9	0.0	0.0	0.0	0.4	0.3	8.2
Peru	18.1	10.2	7.8	2.6	1.4	1.6	0.0	0.6	0.3	6.5
Philippines	26.7	8.2	18.5	2.8	0.0	0.1	0.8	0.4	0.6	19.5
Poland	18.8	11.0	7.8	6.3	0.5	0.1	0.0	0.7	1.1	11.7
Portugal	18.8	15.3	3.5	5.7	0.0	0.0	0.0	0.4	0.3	8.5
Puerto Rico	..	11.2	..	..	0.0	0.0	0.0	..	0.1	..
Qatar	..	..	..	..	..	..	..	..	..	..
Romania	15.5	9.7	5.8	3.6	4.4	0.1	0.0	0.2	1.4	3.3
Russian Federation	37.1	10.0	27.1	3.5	39.6	0.4	0.0	0.6	3.4	–13.4
Rwanda	12.7	7.1	5.6	3.5	0.0	0.0	3.0	0.0	0.2	5.9
Samoa	..	9.5	..	4.0	0.0	0.0	1.8	..	0.3	..
São Tomé and Principe	–3.3	8.0	–11.2	..	0.0	0.0	0.0	..	1.2	..
Saudi Arabia	29.4	10.0	19.5	7.2	51.0	0.0	0.0	1.0	1.2	–26.5
Senegal	11.6	8.1	3.5	3.7	0.0	0.1	0.3	..	0.6	..
Serbia and Montenegro	–2.6	8.7	–11.3	..	2.3	0.3	0.0	0.2	3.5	..
Seychelles	19.5	9.5	10.1	6.3	0.0	0.0	0.0	..	0.2	..
Sierra Leone	2.7	6.4	–3.8	3.9	0.0	0.0	6.3	0.4	0.5	–7.1
Singapore	47.7	14.0	33.7	2.3	0.0	0.0	0.0	0.4	0.4	35.2
Slovak Republic	22.9	11.0	12.0	4.0	0.1	0.0	0.0	0.1	1.1	14.7
Slovenia	23.8	12.0	11.8	5.4	0.0	0.0	0.0	0.2	0.5	16.5
Solomon Islands	..	8.5	..	3.8	0.0	0.1	10.4	..	0.3	..
Somalia	..	..	..	..	..	..	..	..	..	..
South Africa	15.7	13.3	2.4	7.5	0.0	1.0	0.3	0.2	1.6	6.9
Spain	23.0	12.9	10.1	4.4	0.0	0.0	0.0	0.4	0.3	13.7
Sri Lanka	21.9	5.2	16.7	2.9	0.0	0.0	0.5	0.3	0.4	18.4
St. Kitts and Nevis	32.9	12.9	20.0	3.9	0.0	0.0	0.0	..	0.2	..

Country name	Gross national saving	Consumption of fixed capital	Net national saving	Education expenditure	Energy depletion	Mineral depletion	Net forest depletion	PM_{10} damage*	CO_2 damage	Genuine saving
St. Lucia	16.3	11.7	4.6	7.7	0.0	0.0	0.0	..	0.3	..
St. Vincent	19.3	11.1	8.2	4.7	0.0	0.0	0.0	..	0.3	..
Sudan	7.6	9.2	–1.5	0.9	0.0	0.1	0.0	0.6	0.3	–1.6
Suriname	–0.6	9.1	–9.7	..	12.1	2.1	0.0	..	1.4	..
Swaziland	13.4	9.1	4.3	5.1	0.0	0.0	0.0	0.1	0.2	9.1
Sweden	22.3	14.0	8.3	7.7	0.0	0.1	0.0	0.0	0.1	15.8
Switzerland	32.8	14.5	18.3	4.9	0.0	0.0	0.0	0.2	0.1	22.9
Syrian Arab Rep.	24.3	9.6	14.7	3.5	34.5	0.1	0.0	0.8	1.9	–19.1
Taiwan, China	25.6	12.3	13.3	..	0.0	0.0	0.0	..	0.4	..
Tajikistan	1.7	7.0	–5.3	2.0	0.7	0.0	0.0	0.2	2.5	–6.7
Tanzania	12.4	7.4	5.1	2.4	0.0	0.2	0.0	0.2	0.3	6.8
Thailand	30.9	14.9	15.9	3.6	1.6	0.0	0.3	0.4	1.0	16.3
Togo	0.9	7.5	–6.6	4.2	0.0	0.2	4.3	0.3	0.8	–7.9
Tonga	–13.7	9.6	–23.3	4.7	0.0	0.0	0.1	..	0.4	..
Trinidad and Tobago	28.7	12.4	16.3	4.2	29.7	0.0	0.0	0.0	2.1	–11.4
Tunisia	24.3	10.0	14.3	6.4	4.8	0.6	0.2	0.3	0.6	14.1
Turkey	20.1	6.8	13.2	3.1	0.3	0.0	0.0	1.2	0.7	14.1
Turkmenistan	50.5	8.9	41.6	..	182.7	0.0	0.0	0.3	7.7	..
Uganda	15.0	7.3	7.7	1.9	0.0	0.0	6.1	0.0	0.2	3.4
Ukraine	25.6	19.4	6.2	6.4	7.4	0.0	0.0	1.0	6.7	–2.5
United Arab Emirates	..	..	..	..	..	..	..	0.0	..	..
United Kingdom	15.0	11.5	3.5	5.3	1.1	0.0	0.0	0.1	0.2	7.3
United States	17.4	11.7	5.7	4.2	1.2	0.0	0.0	0.3	0.3	8.2
Uruguay	11.2	11.6	–0.4	2.7	0.0	0.0	0.0	1.9	0.2	0.2
Uzbekistan	18.2	8.4	9.8	9.4	42.1	0.0	0.0	0.6	5.2	–28.6
Vanuatu	..	9.8	..	6.9	0.0	0.0	0.0	..	0.2	..
Venezuela, R. B. de	28.5	7.2	21.3	4.4	27.3	0.3	0.0	0.0	0.8	–2.7
Vietnam	31.7	7.9	23.8	2.8	8.7	0.1	1.0	0.4	1.1	15.5
Virgin Islands (U.S.)	..	..	..	..	..	..	..	..	..	..
West Bank and Gaza	–5.5	8.2	–13.6	..	0.0	0.0	0.0	..	..	..
Yemen, Rep. of	34.4	8.9	25.5	..	43.2	0.0	0.0	0.5	0.6	..
Zambia	4.0	7.9	–3.9	2.0	0.0	2.5	0.0	..	0.4	..
Zimbabwe	11.9	8.5	3.3	6.9	0.0	0.6	0.0	0.5	1.3	7.8

Source: Authors.

*Data for particulate matter damage are for 2001.

.. means missing values.

Appendix 4

Change in Wealth per Capita, 2000

Change in Wealth per Capita, 2000, $ per Capita

Country name	GNI per capita	% Population growth rate	Adjusted net saving per capita	Change in wealth per capita	Saving gap % of GNI
Albania	1,220	0.4	145	122	
Algeria	1,670	1.4	–93	–409	24.5
Antigua and Barbuda	8,700	2.0	911	94	
Argentina	7,718	0.9	154	–109	1.4
Australia	19,703	1.1	963	46	
Austria	23,403	0.2	3,032	2,831	
Bangladesh	373	1.7	71	41	
Barbados	9,344	0.3	588	520	
Belgium-Luxembourg	21,756	0.3	2,811	2,649	
Belize	3,230	2.7	303	–150	4.6
Benin	360	2.6	14	–42	11.5
Bhutan	532	2.9	111	–111	20.9
Bolivia	969	2.0	9	–127	13.1
Botswana	2,925	1.7	1,021	814	
Brazil	3,432	1.2	265	64	
Bulgaria	1,504	–1.8	80	238	
Burkina Faso	230	2.5	15	–36	15.8
Burundi	97	1.9	–10	–37	37.7
Cameroon	548	2.2	–8	–152	27.7
Canada	22,612	0.9	3,006	2,221	
Cape Verde	1,195	2.7	43	–81	6.8

Country name	GNI per capita	% Population growth rate	Adjusted net saving per capita	Change in wealth per capita	Saving gap % of GNI
Chad	174	3.1	–8	–74	42.6
Chile	4,779	1.3	406	129	
China	844	0.7	236	200	
Colombia	1,926	1.7	–6	–205	10.6
Comoros	367	2.5	–17	–73	19.9
Congo, Rep. of	660	3.2	–227	–727	110.2
Costa Rica	3,857	2.1	464	107	
Côte d'Ivoire	625	2.3	–5	–100	16.0
Denmark	29,009	0.4	4,376	4,014	
Dominica	3,344	–0.3	–53	7	
Dominican Republic	2,234	1.6	341	198	
Ecuador	1,170	1.5	–51	–293	25.1
Egypt, Arab Rep. of	1,569	1.9	91	–45	2.9
El Salvador	2,075	1.5	113	37	
Estonia	3,836	–0.5	570	681	
Ethiopia	101	2.4	–4	–27	27.1
Fiji	2,055	1.4	–23	–109	5.3
Finland	22,893	0.1	4,334	4,236	
France	22,399	0.5	3,249	2,951	
Gabon	3,370	2.3	–1,183	–2,241	66.5
Gambia, The	305	3.4	–5	–45	14.6
Georgia	601	–0.5	4	16	
Germany	22,641	0.1	2,180	2,071	
Ghana	255	1.7	16	–18	7.2
Greece	10,706	0.3	1,431	1,327	
Grenada	3,671	0.7	650	533	
Guatemala	1,676	2.6	37	–123	7.3
Guyana	870	0.4	–49	–108	12.4
Haiti	503	2.0	133	106	
Honduras	897	2.6	213	53	
Hungary	4,370	–0.4	676	765	
India	446	1.7	67	16	
Indonesia	675	1.3	20	–56	8.4

Country name	GNI per capita	% Population growth rate	Adjusted net saving per capita	Change in wealth per capita	Saving gap % of GNI
Iran, Islamic Rep. of	1,580	1.5	–142	–398	25.2
Ireland	21,495	1.3	4,964	4,199	
Israel	17,354	2.6	1,540	268	
Italy	18,478	0.1	1,990	1,947	
Jamaica	2,954	0.8	471	371	
Japan	37,879	0.2	5,906	5,643	
Jordan	1,727	3.1	236	28	
Kenya	343	2.3	40	–11	3.2
Korea, Rep. of	10,843	0.8	2,694	2,415	
Latvia	3,271	–0.8	412	551	
Madagascar	245	3.1	9	–56	22.7
Malawi	162	2.1	–2	–29	18.2
Malaysia	3,554	2.4	767	227	
Mali	221	2.4	20	–47	21.2
Mauritania	382	2.9	–30	–147	38.4
Mauritius	3,697	1.1	645	514	
Mexico	5,783	1.4	545	155	
Moldova	316	–0.2	38	56	
Morocco	1,131	1.6	200	117	
Mozambique	195	2.2	15	–20	10.0
Namibia	1,820	3.2	392	140	
Nepal	239	2.4	46	2	
Netherlands	23,382	0.7	3,673	3,176	
New Zealand	12,679	0.6	1,550	1,082	
Nicaragua	739	2.6	81	–18	2.4
Niger	166	3.3	–10	–83	50.3
Nigeria	297	2.4	–97	–210	70.6
Norway	36,800	0.7	6,916	5,708	
Pakistan	517	2.4	54	–2	0.4
Panama	3,857	1.5	829	585	
Paraguay	1,465	2.3	131	–93	6.4
Peru	1,991	1.5	148	15	
Philippines	1,033	2.3	211	114	

Country name	GNI per capita	% Population growth rate	Adjusted net saving per capita	Change in wealth per capita	Saving gap % of GNI
Portugal	10,256	0.6	943	750	
Romania	1,639	–0.1	80	89	
Russian Federation	1,738	–0.5	–164	4	
Rwanda	233	2.9	14	–60	26.0
Senegal	449	2.6	31	–27	6.1
Seychelles	7,089	0.9	1,162	904	
Singapore	22,968	1.7	8,258	6,949	
South Africa	2,837	2.5	246	–2	0.1
Spain	13,723	0.7	1,987	1,663	
Sri Lanka	868	1.4	166	116	
St. Kitts and Nevis	6,746	4.7	1,612	–63	0.9
St. Lucia	4,103	1.5	507	253	
St. Vincent	2,824	0.2	365	336	
Swaziland	1,375	2.5	129	8	
Sweden	26,809	0.1	4,278	4,191	
Switzerland	37,165	0.6	8,611	8,020	
Syrian Arab Republic	1,064	2.5	–175	–473	44.5
Thailand	1,989	0.8	351	259	
Togo	285	4.0	–20	–88	30.8
Trinidad and Tobago	5,838	0.5	–541	–774	13.3
Tunisia	1,936	1.1	291	176	
Turkey	2,980	1.7	476	273	
United Kingdom	24,606	0.3	1,882	1,725	
United States	35,188	1.1	3,092	2,020	
Uruguay	5,962	0.6	137	20	
Venezuela, R. B. de	4,970	1.8	–94	–847	17.0
Zambia	312	2.0	–13	–63	20.4
Zimbabwe	550	2.0	53	–4	0.7

Source: Authors.
Note: Countries with saving gap are those with negative changes in wealth per capita.

References

Adams, Richard H. Jr., and John Page. 2003. "International Migration, Remittances and Poverty in Developing Countries." Policy Research Working Paper 3179, World Bank, Washington DC.

Aronsson T., P.-O. Johansson, K.-G. Lofgren. 1997. *Welfare Measurement, Sustainability and Green National Accounting.* Cheltenham: Edward Elgar Publishing Ltd.

Arrow, K. J., P. Dasgupta, and K.-G. Mäler. 2003a. "Evaluating Projects and Assessing Sustainable Development in Imperfect Economies." *Environmental and Resource Economics* 26 (4): 647–85.

———. 2003b. "The Genuine Savings Criterion and the Value of Population." *Economic Theory* 21(2–3): 217–25.

Arrow, K. J., and others. 2004. "Are We Consuming Too Much?" *Journal of Economic Perspectives* 18 (3): 147–72.

Atkinson, G., and K. Hamilton. 2003. "Savings, Growth and the Resource Curse Hypothesis." *World Development* 31:1793–1807.

Australian Bureau of Statistics. 1999. *Consolidated Balance Sheet.* ABS: Canberra.

Auty, Richard M., ed. 2001. *Resource Abundance and Economic Development.* Oxford: Oxford University Press.

Barro R., and J. W. Lee. 2000. "International Data on Educational Attainment: Updates and Implications." CID Working Paper 42, Center for International Development, Harvard University, Cambridge MA.

Bartelmus, P., E. Lutz, and S. Schweinfest. 1992. "Integrated Environmental and Economic Accounting: A Case Study for Papua-New Guinea." Environmental Working Paper 54, World Bank, Washington, DC.

Bartelmus P., and A. Vesper. 2000. "Green accounting and material flow analysis: Alternatives or complements?" *Wuppertal Institute Paper* No. 106.

Beck, T., A. Demirgüç-Kunt, and R. Levine. 1999. "A New Database on Financial Development and Structure." *World Bank Economic Review* 14 (3): 597–605.

Becker, G. S. 1964. *Human Capital: A Theoretical and Empirical Analysis, With Special Reference to Education.* New York: National Bureau of Economic Research (NBER), Columbia University Press.

Behrman, Jere R., and Paul J. Taubman. 1982. "Human Capital." In *Encyclopedia of Economics,* ed. Douglas Greenwald, 474–76. New York: McGraw-Hill Book Company.

Berndt, E. R., and B. C. Field., eds. 1981. *Modeling and Measuring Natural Resource Substitution.* Cambridge MA: MIT Press.

Berry L., J. Olson, and D. Campbell. 2003. "Assessing the Extent, Cost and Impact of Land Degradation at the National Level: Findings and Lessons Learned from Seven Pilot Countries." Photocopy. Paper commissioned by the Global Mechanism of the UN Commission to Combat Desertification. Rome: Global Mechanism of the UNCCD.

Bjorklund, Anders, and Christian Kjellstrom. 2002. "Estimating the Return to Investments in Education: How Useful Is the Standard Mincer Equation?" *Economics of Education Review* 21: 195–210.

Blignaut, J. N.; R. M. Hassan. 2001. "A Natural Resource Accounting Analysis of the Contribution of Mineral Resources to Sustainable Development in South Africa." *South African Journal of Economic and Management Sciences,* N.S. v0, n.0 (Supplement April 2001)

Bohm, B., A. Gleiss, M. Wagner, and D. Ziegler. 2002. "Dissagregated Capital Stock Estimation for Austria—Methods, Concepts and Results." *Applied Economics* 34: 23–37.

Caselli, F. Forthcoming. "The Missing Input: Accounting for Cross-Country Income Differences." In *Handbook of Economic Growth,* ed. P. Aghion and S. Durlauf. Amsterdam: North Holland.

Chang, K. 1994. "Capital-Energy Substitution and the Multi-Level CES Production Function." *Energy Economics* 16 (1): 22–26.

Chiang, A. C. 1984. *Fundamental Methods of Mathematical Economics.* 3rd edition. Singapore: McGraw-Hill Book Company.

Croitoru L., P. Gatto, M. Merlo, and P. Paiero., ed. 2005. *Valuing Mediterranean Forests—Towards the Total Economic Value.* Rome: CABI Publishing.

Dasgupta, P. 2001. *Human Well-Being and the Natural Environment.* Oxford: Oxford University Press.

Dasgupta, P., and K.-G. Mäler. 2000. "Net National Product, Wealth, and Social Well-Being. *Environment and Development Economics* 5: 69–93.

De Boer, B., M. de Haan, and M. Voogt. 1994. "What would Net Domestic Product have been in an environmentally sustainable economy?" Presented in Papers and Proceedings of the Meeting on National Accounts and the Environment, 16-18 March, London.

Desaulty, D. and P. Templé. 1999. "In 1997, France Spent 145 Billion Francs on Environmental Protection." *Les données de l'environnement—Economie,* No. 46, Orleans: Institut Français de l'Environnement.

Dixit A., P. Hammond, and M. Hoel. 1980. "On Hartwick's Rule for Regular Maximum Paths of Capital Accumulation and Resource Depletion." *Review of Economic Studies* 47 (3): 551–56.

Dixon, J., K. Hamilton, and A. Kunte. 1997. "Measuring the Wealth of Nations," Expanding the Measure of Wealth: Indicators of Environmentally Sustainable Development. *Environmentally Sustainable Development Studies and Monographs,* Series 17. Washington, DC: World Bank.

ENRAP (Environment and Natural Resources Accounting Project). 1999. *ENRAP-SHELF (Searchable Hyperlink Electronic Library of Files) CD-ROM.* CD containing all accounts and technical reports from the Philippine Environmental and Natural Resource Accounting Project. Manila: ENRAP.

Eurostat. 2000. *Accounts for Sub-Soil Assets: Results of Pilot Studies in European Countries.* Luxembourg: Eurostat.

———. 2002. *Natural Resource Accounts for Forests.* Detailed Tables. Luxembourg: European Communities.

Fankhauser, S. 1994. "The Social Costs of Greenhouse Gas Emissions: An Expected Value Approach." *Energy Journal* 15 (2): 157–84.

Ferreira, S., K. Hamilton, and J. Vincent. 2003. "Comprehensive Wealth and Future Consumption." Photocopy. World Bank, Washington, DC.

Ferreira, S., and J. Vincent. 2005. "Genuine Savings: Leading Indicator of Sustainable Development?" *Economic Development and Cultural Change* 53: 737–54.

Fisher, I. 1906. *Nature of Capital and Income.* New York: Macmillan.

Fortech—Dames & Moore Company. 1997. "Marketing of PNG Forest Products Milestone 2 Project: Logging and Processing Costs in Papua New Guinea." Australia: Forestry Technical Services Pty, Ltd.

Global Witness. 2001. "Taylor-made: The Pivotal Role of Liberia's Forests and Flag of Convenience in Regional Conflict." United Kingdom: Global Witness Limited. http://www.globalwitness.org/campaigns/forests/liberia/downloads/taylormade2.pdf

Greene, W. 2000. *Econometric Analysis.* 4th edition. Upper Saddle River, NJ: Prentice Hall.

Gretton, Paul, and Umme Salma. 1996. "Land Degradation and the Australian Agricultural Industry." Industry Commission Staff Information Paper, Government of Australia, Camberra.

Gylfason, Thorvaldur. 2001. "Natural Resources, Education and Economic Development." *European Economic Review* 45: 847–59.

Hamilton, K. 1994. "Green Adjustments to GDP." *Resources Policy* 20 (3): 155–68.

———. 1995. "Sustainable Development, the Hartwick Rule and Optimal Growth." *Environmental and Resource Economics* 5: 393–411.

———. 2000. "Greening the National Accounts: Formal Models and Practical Measurement." In *Greening the Accounts,* ed. J. L. R. Proops and S. Simon. Cheltenham, U.K.: Edward Elgar Publishers.

———. 2005. "Testing Genuine Saving." Policy Research Working Paper 3577, World Bank, Washington, DC.

Hamilton, K., and M. Clemens. 1999. "Genuine Savings Rates in Developing Countries." *World Bank Economic Review* 13 (2): 333–56.

Hamilton, K., and J. M. Hartwick. 2005. "Investing Exhaustible Resource Rents and the Path of Consumption." *Canadian Journal of Economics* 38 (2): 615–21.

Hamilton, K., and C. Withagen. 2004. "Savings, Welfare and Rules for Sustainability." Photocopy. World Bank, Washington, DC.

Hamilton, K., G. Ruta, and L. Tajibaeva. Forthcoming. "Capital Accumulation and Resource Depletion: A Hartwick Rule Counterfactual." *Environmental and Resource Economics.*

Haripriya, G.S. 1998. "Forest Resource Accounting: Preliminary Estimates for the State of Maharashtra." *Development Policy Review* 16: 131–51.

Hartwick, John M. 1977. "Intergenerational Equity and the Investing of Rents from Exhaustible Resources." *American Economic Review* 66: 972–74.

Hicks, J. R. 1946. *Value and Capital.* 2nd Edition. Oxford: Oxford University Press.

Hnatkovska, V., and N. Loayza. 2004. "Volatility and Growth." In *Managing Volatility and Crises: A Practitioner's Guide,* ed. B. Pinto and others. Washington, DC: World Bank.

Jorgensen, D. W. and B. M. Fraumeni. 1992. "The Output of the Education Sector." In Zvi Griliches, ed., *Output Measurement in the Service Sectors.* Chicago: University of Chicago Press."

Jorgensen, Dale W., and Eric Yip. 2001. "Whatever Happened to Productivity Growth." In *New Developments in Productivity Analysis,* ed. Charles R. Hulten, Edwin R. Dean, and J. Michael Harper. NBER Studies in Income and Wealth 63. Chicago and London: University of Chicago Press.

Kaufmann, D., A. Kraay, and M. Mastruzzi. 2005. "Governance Matters IV: Governance Indicators for 1996–2004." Policy Research Working Paper 3630, World Bank, Washington DC.

Kemfert, C. 1998. "Estimated Production Elasticities of a Nested CES Production Function Approach for Germany." *Energy Economics* 20: 249–64.

Kemfert, C., and H. Welsch. 2000. "Energy-Capital-Labor Substitution and the Economic Effects of CO_2 Abatement: Evidence for Germany." *Journal of Policy Modeling* 22 (6): 641–60.

Kent, A. 1972. "Optimal Growth When the Stock of Resources is Finite and Depletable." *Journal of Economic Theory* 4 (2): 256–67.

Kunte, A., K. Hamilton, J. Dixon, and M. Clemens. 1998. "Estimating National Wealth: Methodology and Results." Environment Department Paper 57, World Bank, Washington, DC.

Lampietti, J., and J. Dixon. 1995. "To See the Forest for the Trees: A Guide to Non-Timber Forest Benefits." Environment Department Paper 13. World Bank, Washington DC.

Lange, G.-M. 1997. "Strategic Planning for Sustainable Development in Indonesia Using Natural Resource Accounts." In *Economy and Ecosystems in Change: Analytical and Historical Approaches,* ed. J. van den Bergh and J. van der Straaten. Aldershott, U.K.: Edward Elgar Publishing.

———. 2000a. "The Contribution of Minerals to Sustainable Economic Development in Botswana." Report to the Botswana Natural Resource Accounting Programme, National Conservation Strategy Agency and Ministry of Finance, Central Statistics Office. Gaborone, Botswana.

———. 2000b. "The Use and Policy Applications of the Philippine System of Environmental and Natural Resource Accounts." Report for the Philippines National Statistical Coordinating Board. Manila.

———. 2003a. "Fisheries Accounting in Namibia." In *Natural Resource Accounting and Economic Development: Theory and Practice,* ed. C. Perrings and J. Vincent. Cheltenham, U.K.: Edward Elgar Publishers.

———. 2003b. "Policy Application of Environmental Accounting." Environment Department Paper 88. Washington DC: World Bank.

Lange, G., and D.J. Motinga. 1997. "The Contribution of Resource Rents from Minerals and Fisheries to Sustainable Economic Development in Namibia, 1980 to 1995. Research Discussion Paper 19. Directorate of Environmental Affairs, Ministry of Environment and Tourism: Windhoek, Namibia.

Lange, G.-M., J. Arntzen, S. Kabaija, and M. Monamati. 2000. "Botswana's Natural Resource Accounts: The Case of Water." Report to the Botswana Natural Resource Accounting Programme, National Conservation Strategy Agency and Ministry of Finance, Central Statistics Office. Gaborone, Botswana.

Lange, G.M., R. Hassan, and K. Hamilton. 2003. *Environmental Accounting in Action: Case Studies from Southern Africa.* Cheltenham: Edward Elgar Publishing.

Lange, G.-M., and M. Wright. 2004. "Sustainable Development in Mineral Economies: the Example of Botswana." *Environment and Development Economics* 9 (4): 485–505.

Larson, Donald F., Rita Butzer, Yair Mundlak, and Al Crego. 2000. "A Cross-Country Database for Sector Investment and Capital." *The World Bank Economic Review* 14 (2): 371–91.

Lopina, Olga, Andrei Ptichnikov, and Alexander Voropayev. 2003. *Illegal Logging in Northwestern Russia and Exports of Russian Forest Products to Sweden*. Russia: World Wildlife Fund.

Manne, A., and R. Richels. 1992. *Buying Greenhouse Insurance: The Economic Costs of* CO_2 *Emission Limits*. Cambridge MA: MIT Press.

Mas, Matilde, Francisco Perez, and Ezequiel Uriel. 2000. "Estimation of the Stock of Capital in Spain." *Review of Income and Wealth* 46 (1): 103–16.

Mitra, T. 1978. "Efficient Growth with Exhaustible Resources in a Neoclassical Model." *Journal of Economic Theory* 17 (1): 114–29.

Millennium Ecosystem Assessment. 2005. *Ecosystems and Human Well-Being: Synthesis.* Washington, DC: Island Press.

NIER (National Institute for Economic Research). 2000. *Environmental Impacts of Swedish Trade-Results of a pilot study.* Stockholm.

O'Connor, M. 2000. "Toward a Typology of Environmentally-Adjusted National Sustainability Indicators: Key Concepts and Policy Applications." Working Paper 95.2000. Milano: Fondazione Eni Enrico Mattei.

Paldam, Martin, and Gert Tinggaard Svendsen. Forthcoming. "Social Capital Database for a Cross-Country Study." In *Trust, Social Capital and Economic Growth: an International Comparison,* ed. M. Paldam and G. T. Svendsen. Cheltenham, U.K.: Edward Elgar Publishing.

Pandey, K., K. Bolt, U. Deichman, K. Hamilton, B. Ostro, and D. Wheeler. 2005."The Human Cost of Air Pollution: New Estimates for Developing Countries." Development Research Group and Environment Department, World Bank, Washington, DC.

Pearce, D. W. 1993. "Blueprint 3: Measuring Sustainable Development." Earthscan: London.

Pearce, D. W., and G. Atkinson. 1993. "Capital Theory and the Measurement of Sustainable Development: An Indicator of Weak Sustainability." *Ecological Economics* 8 (2): 103–108.

Pearce, D. W., and D. Ulph. 1999. "A Social Discount Rate for the United Kingdom." In *Environmental Economics: Essays in Ecological Economics and Sustainable Development,* ed. D. W. Pearce, 268–285. Cheltenham: Edward Elgar Publishing.

Pezzey, J. 1989. "Economic Analysis of Sustainable Growth and Sustainable Development." Environment Department Working Paper 15, World Bank, Washington, DC.

Pritchett, L. 1996. "Where Has All the Education Gone?" Policy Research Working Paper 1581, World Bank, Washington, DC.

———. 2000. "The Tyranny of Concepts: CUDIE (Cumulated, Depreciated, Investment Effort) is *Not* Capital." *Journal of Economic Growth* 5 (December): 361–84.

Prywes, M. 1986. "A Nested CES Approach to Capital-Energy Substitution." *Energy Economics* 8: 22–28.

Psacharopoulos, George, and Harry Anthony Patrinos. 2004. "Returns to Investment in Education: A Further Update." *Education Economics* 12 (2): 111–34.

Repetto, R., W. Magrath, M. Wells, C. Beer, and F. Rossini. 1989. *Wasting Assets: Natural Resources in the National Accounts.* Washington: World Resources Institute.

Rosengrant, M. W., M. Agcaoili-Sombilla, and N.D. Perez. 1995. "Global Food Projections to 2020: Implications for Investment." Food, Agriculture, and the Environment Discussion Paper 5, International Food Policy Research Institute, Washington DC.

Sachs, J., and A. Warner. 1995. "Natural Resource Abundance and Economic Growth." Development Discussion Paper 517a. Harvard Institute for International Development, Cambridge, MA.

Sala-i-Martin, X. 1997. "I Just Ran Two Million Regressions." *American Economic Review* 87 (2): 178–183.

Samuelson, P. 1961. "The Evaluation of 'Social Income': Capital Formation and Wealth." In F. A. Lutz and D. C. Hague (eds.), *The Theory of Capital.* New York: St. Martin's Press.

Sarraf, M., and M. Jiwanji. 2001. "Beating the Resource Curse: The Case of Botswana." Environment Department Working Paper 83, Environmental Economics Series, World Bank, Washington, DC.

Schultz, T. W. 1961. "Investments in Human Capital." *American Economic Review* 51 (1): 1–17.

Schultz, T. P. 1988. "Education Investments and Returns." In *Handbook of Development Economics,* Volume 1, ed. H. Chenery and T. N. Srinivasan. Amsterdam: Elsevier Science Publishers, B.V.

Smith, Adam. 1776. *An Inquiry into the Nature and Causes of the Wealth of Nations.* Chicago: University of Chicago Press, 1977.

Solow, R. 1986. "On the Intergenerational Allocation of Natural Resources." *Scandinavian Journal of Economics* 88 (1): 141–49.

Sorensen, K. and J. Hass. 1998. Norwegian Economic and Environmental Accounts Project. Statistics Norway: Oslo.

Statistics Canada. 2000. "Agricultural Land Use and Supply." Ottawa: Statistics Canada.

Stiglitz, J. E. 1974a. "Growth with Exhaustible Natural Resources: Efficient and Optimal Growth Paths." Symposium on the Economics of Exhaustible Resources. *Review of Economic Studies* 41: 123–37.

———. 1974b. "Growth with Exhaustible Natural Resources: The Competitive Economy." Symposium on the Economics of Exhaustible Resources. *Review of Economic Studies* 41: 139–52.

Tay, John, John Healey, and Colin Price. 2001. "Financial Assessment of Reduced Impact Logging Techniques in Sabah, Malaysia." In *Applying Reduced Impact Logging to Advanced Sustainable Forest Management.* Bangkok, Thailand: UNFAO.

Tol, R. 2005. "The Marginal Damage Cost of Carbon Dioxide Emissions: An Assessment of the Uncertainties." *Energy Policy* 33: 2064–2074.

United Nations. 1993. *Integrated Environmental and Economic Accounting.* Series F 61. New York: United Nations.

———. 2000. *Handbook of National Accounting: Integrated Environmental and Economic Accounting—An Operational Manual.* New York: United Nations.

———. 2003. *Handbook of National Accounting: Integrated Environmental and Economic Accounting—An Operational Manual.* New York: United Nations.

UNFAO (United Nations Food and Agriculture Organization). 2000. "Global Forest Resources Assessment 2000: Main Report." Forestry Paper 140, Rome, UNFAO.

USGS (U.S. Geological Survey). 2005. *Mineral Commodity Summaries.* Washington, DC: U.S. Government Printing Office.

———. Web page: www.usgs.gov.

van der Hout, Peter. 2000. "Testing the Applicability of Reduced Impact Logging in Greenheart Forest in Guyana." *International Forestry Review* 2 (1). Oxford: Commonwealth Forestry Association.

van Tongeren, J., S. Schweinfest, and E. Lutz. 1991. "Integrated Environmental and Economic Accounting: A Case Study of Mexico." Environment Working Paper 50, World Bank, Washington, DC.

Verbruggen, H., R. Dellink, R. Gerlagh, and M. Hofkes. 2000. "Calculations of a sustainable national income: Four variants." In H. Verbruggen, ed., *Final Report on Calculations of a Sustainable National Income according to Hueting's Methodology.* Institute for Environmental Studies. Vrije Universiteit: Amsterdam, The Netherlands.

Vincent, J. 1996. "Resource Depletion and Economic Sustainability in Malaysia." Development Discussion Paper 542, Harvard Institute for International Development, Cambridge, MA.

Wagner, G. 2004. "Environmental Macroeconomics Bibliography." Available at http://www.gwagner.net/work/environmental macroeconomics.html.

Ward, M. 1976. *The Measurement of Capital: The Methodology of Capital Stock Estimates in OECD Countries.* Paris: OECD.

Weitzman, M. L. 1976. "On the Welfare Significance of National Product in a Dynamic Economy." *Quarterly Journal of Economics* 90 (1): 156–62.

Weitzman, M.L. and K.-G. Löfgren. 1997. On the Welfare Significance of Green Accounting as Taught by Parable, *Journal of Environmental Economics and Management* 32: 139-53.

Whiteman, Adrian. 1996. "Economic Rent and the Appropriate Level of Forest Products Royalties in 1996." Jakarta, Indonesia: U.K. Tropical Forest Management Programme, Jakarta, Indonesia.

World Bank. 1996. *Monitoring Environmental Progress: A Report on Work in Progress.* Washington, DC: World Bank.

World Bank. 1997. *Expanding the Measure of Wealth: Indicators of Environmentally Sustainable Development.* Environmentally Sustainable Development Studies and Monographs Series No. 17. Washington, DC: World Bank.

———. 2002. *World Development Indicators 2002.* Washington, DC: World Bank.

———. 2004. *World Development Indicators 2004.* Washington, DC: World Bank.

———. 2005. *World Development Indicators 2005.* Washington, DC: World Bank.

World Commission on the Environment and Development (WCED). 1987. *Our Common Future.* Oxford: Oxford University Press.

WRI (World Resources Institute). 2000. *The Weight of Nations: Material Outflows from Industrial Economies.* Washington DC.

Index

Boxes, figures, and tables are indicated by b, f, and t.